Shamu, Splash & Solemn

by Anne Gerber and Emilio DeGrazia

The Creative Writing of
Carole Jayne Stoa Senn

SHIPWRECKT BOOKS PUBLISHING COMPANY
Lost Lake Folk Art
Rushford, Minnesota

Editorial & Design Assistance by Jill Krase
Additional Cover, Graphic & Interior Design by
Shipwreckt Books

Notice: *All of the contributions of Carole Stoa Senn to this book were facilitated by the book's co-authors, Anne Gerber and Emilio DeGrazia. Carole will in no way profit from any sales generated by publication of this book. Carole has requested that the publisher and co-authors donate one-third of all proceeds from sales of this book to her favorite non-profit organization, Minnesota Public Radio. The co-authors and publisher of Shipwreckt Books are pleased to honor this request.*

Copyright © 2017 Anne Gerber and Emilio DeGrazia
Copyright © 2017 Lost Lake Folk Art
All rights reserved
ISBN-10: 0-9968909-2-0
ISBN-13:978-0-9968909-2-2

You know quite well, deep within you,
That there is only a single magic,
A single power,
A single salvation…
And that is called loving.

Well then, love your suffering.
Do not resist it, do not flee from it.
It is only your aversion to it that hurts,
And nothing else.

Hermann Hesse

Table of Contents

A Single Power, A Single Salvation by Emilio DeGrazia	1
Like Churchbells from Childhood	23
Carole's Memoir 2010–2012 and Poems 1992–1993	
Prairie Breeze	25
Color Wheel	31
The Sun, the Moon and the Thunderstorm	37
Dressage	41
Coma: The Nina, the Pinta, and the Santa Maria	45
The Recovery	47
"Golden Valley"	49
The Blue Moon Rose and Burgundy Rose	53
Horsemen's Horseman—Hans Senn	57
A Celebration of Hans' Life by Sandra Knaeble	57
Love Song	61
A Woman's Voice Keeps Haunting Me	65
Carole's Journal 1994–1995	
The Making of Carole's Memoir	85
Anne Gerber	
Writing One of Carole's Dreams	103
Carole's Poems: 2013–2017	109
Thinking in Poems	133
Sent from Carole's iPad	
Special Acknowledgment from Carole	137

A Single Power, A Single Salvation
by Emilio DeGrazia

In a culture that finds success stories profitable, it is customary to celebrate free will while ignoring what the preacher in the Book of Ecclesiastes says: "Time and chance happeneth to us all." The main character in a typical success story is a strong-willed individual who overcomes adversity to achieve a happy ending that features such rewards as a true love, a happy marriage, and a prosperity not subject to the whims of circumstance. In those narratives, happy endings usually happen before the hero or heroine gets divorced, sick, or old.

What follows in these pages—Carole's story—is a necessarily fragmented account of how a talented and lovely young life was ravaged twice by violent attacks against which she had no way to defend herself. As defenseless victim she twice learned how "time and chance" could impose staggering afflictions that disabled her in important ways. But hers is also a "success" story about how an almost physically helpless and almost invisible woman created a life for herself out of the outrageous circumstances that singled her out. It is in part a story about the power of the small compassionate work of a few friends and family, the power of the mysterious and resilient mind, and the power of imagination to recreate a life.

Carole would put horses, rather than herself, at the center of this story. When Carole, as a ninth grader, acquired her first horse, Wade's Falcon, she could not have foreseen how important horses or the original owner of Wade's Falcon, Hans Senn, would become to her. Hers is in part the story of how the beauty, poetry, and power of horses helped redeem a life.

Carole first appeared in my life in the spring of 1975. I see her there now—sitting rather dutifully upright just to my right—in the front row of an American literature class I was teaching at Winona State College (now Winona State University). As I stood before the class for the first time and surveyed twenty-eight students in their chairs I caught a glimpse of Carole looking up at me, attentive and a bit scared; and as my eyes passed hers, she smiled. She was Carole Stoa then, daughter of a prominent family in Winona, a town of about 25,000 on the Minnesota side of the Mississippi River. Her father, I eventually learned, was president of a local bank, her sister Helen had been named Miss Winona and had presided as queen over the town's Steamboat Days festivities, and her brother Tom was conducting a door-to-door campaign that resulted in his being elected to the Minnesota State Legislature in 1976. She had a loving mother, Merle, and another supportive brother, Jim. She had solid Midwestern roots, good beginnings, the right stuff for the making of success.

Like most professors who see their students coming and going from classes as shoppers picking up electives at a supermarket, I lost Carole in the crowd. What I knew about most students came from what they revealed in the papers they wrote and comments they made in class. Carole was a conscientious student and a lucid, well-organized writer, but she seldom let words pass through the smile that illuminated her face whenever a question came her way. What did become clear was that American literature was speaking to her, especially some of its poets.

I gave her a well-earned 'B' in the class. I was pleased to see her in the front row again a few months later, this time in an upper-division summer school course on modern American literature. In that class was a brilliant young woman named Margaret Tweedy, daughter of a well-known Winona physician. Carole and Margaret had known each other at Winona Senior High School, and their mutual interest in literature deepened their bond. Margaret was full of subtle wit and expressed it with gentle good humor; Carole responded to Margaret with her gracious smiles. Carole seldom spoke, relying on her smile and penetrating eyes to connect with others. Silence seemed a world she lived in comfortably.

She received a well-deserved 'A'.

Then, like almost all students who disappear from professors' lives after brief stays for a course or two, Carole became an absentee. In the summer of 1978, Margaret informed me that Carole was dating Sabon Crook, a young man from Wisconsin. A bit later she surprised me with the news that Carole had married him. She was living on a farm in Westby, Wisconsin, and they were raising goats.

She and Sabon showed up at my house one day. They were selling goat cheeses—large yellowish balls the size of honeydew melons. Carole did not look like a banker's daughter as she carried the goat cheese balls in from the car. She was wearing roughed-up jeans, a plain print shirt, and scruffy boots. She was a goat farmer.

Carole in the 1970s

I never really liked the goat cheese, but every few weeks Carole and Sabon would bring two more. I of course was wondering: What kind of life was she leading? Living on a farm in the rolling hills near Westby certainly had a romantic allure, but the young couple seemed poor. Would their bucolic romance survive the economic demands made of them? And what about Carole's love of literature? What could she do with it on a goat farm? Her friend Margaret had volunteered to be an assistant editor for *Great River Review*, the new regional literary magazine

I had just founded. Would Carole sustain and develop her interest in literature among the goats?

"Are you reading?" I asked her on one of her goat cheese runs.

"Yes, lots," she replied simply, with one of her smiles.

"Are you writing?"

"Yes, poetry."

"Will you let me see some of your poems?" I asked.

Her response was a smile that now seems permanent to me.

Then she was gone again, and then there were no more goat cheese deliveries, and no poems in the mail.

"Have you heard from Carole?" I asked Margaret one day.

Things were not going smoothly, Margaret said, and she didn't know why.

In the spring of 1981 Carole and Sabon divorced. But rural life still had allure, as did a fourteen-horse stable named Prairie Breeze owned by Jay Jackson. In January of 1985 Carole entered into a second marriage, hoping to begin a new life in a place where she and her new husband could board horses. Carole relocated to the idyllic Driftless area near Decorah in northeastern Iowa, and moved her belongings into a small farm house owned by her mother-in-law Marge. She also entered into a relationship that proved disastrous.

Marge's issues with alcohol took its toll on the new couple, and other problems soon became apparent. Carole recalls that Jay (in her words) "had a mental disorder [that was] not diagnosed but could be felt." There were angry outbursts and "harsh words that broke down my character." Carole had her horses, but what came with them was a terrible marriage relationship.

One avenue of escape from her bad marriage was Orval Harris Bucker, who farmed not far from Prairie Breeze. With Orval, Carole shared her passion for "horses, farming, and good conversation." There is reason to suspect that husband Jay became violently jealous. There were attempts to heal the hurts. After participating in therapy sessions for alcoholic family members, Carole took up residence at Helvetia Stables near Stillwater, Minnesota, owned by Hans Senn, the Swiss native who had sold the Stoa family Wade's Falcon, her first horse. At Helvetia, Hans gave Carole a respite that came from grooming, training, and riding the horses she loved. As a trusted friend,

Hans understood that Carole's marriage was troubled, and he gave her time and space to rethink her life with Jay.

Then on November 26, 1986, Carole returned to Prairie Breeze for the Thanksgiving holiday. She noticed that Jay was acting strange, and "needed to talk to her." On that fateful day, Jay cornered Carole in his pickup truck and began firing shots at her. Carole managed to leap from the truck into a cornfield, with Jay giving chase. He then tried several times to run her over with his truck, and, finally, he turned the gun on himself.

Carole staggered to a roadside. From there she was rushed by ambulance to Winneshiek County Hospital and then transferred by helicopter to the Mayo Clinic's St. Mary's Hospital in Rochester, Minnesota. An examination revealed that Jay had shot her six times, then inflicted other injuries by trying to run her over with his truck. She was a fortunate victim: She had the incredible good luck of having two of the six bullets buffered by her heavy jacket. Her wounds were treated at St. Mary's Hospital and she underwent orthopedic surgery for a fractured radius. Thus, Carole began a long and hard journey too familiar to women victims of domestic violence.

Carole was discharged from St. Mary's in December 1986, with a Mayo Clinic orthopedic doctor monitoring her developments. She returned home to her parents in Winona, where she began recovering from the ordeal. Then, in early 1987, she moved into Hans Senn's Helvetia Stables. With Hans as supportive friend, she began developing her own business of breaking horses. Because she was still unable to ride, she hired another woman to help with some of the functions she could not do because of her injuries. By early March 1987, her Mayo Clinic orthopedic doctor was pleased enough with her progress to allow her to resume her normal functions, including lifting and riding. Though she had been attending counseling sessions in nearby White Bear Lake, she stopped visiting with her counselor in April of the same year. She was "too busy" and had resumed her work, and riding, at Hans' Helvetia Stables.

On July 7, 1989, Carole's Decorah friend Orval died in a farm accident.

I had not seen Carole in several years and knew nothing about the troubles in her life. On a sunny day in November 1991, I looked up to see a stranger standing just outside my office door. The Carole who entered and took a seat next to my desk was tentative and gaunt, and the calm of her face was gone. The young woman who once seemed too innocently shy to speak now appeared too helpless to do anything but fix me with her eyes as they filled with tears. She responded to my questions with nods, and could not find words. I coaxed words from her. Yes, she said at last, her husband had shot her. Six times. She crawled away. She told me there was a bullet still lodged in her neck. She was living with Hans. She was riding again. She was trying to be okay.

She was trying to write poetry.

And though I knew that many Vietnam War veterans were afflicted by post-traumatic stress disorder it did not occur to me until later that Carole was also struggling with it.

Would I look at her poetry?

Yes, she should send her poems to me. But she'd have to promise to spend some time every day writing more poems. More than a few times the professor of literature in me had presumed to be a psychiatrist too, for students who turned to me for consolation, explanations, or advice. Too often I responded without carefully listening, and I often had easy answers for them. Why had Carole returned to me in her dark time? She needed, and struggled, to speak. It was like writing poetry. Poetry, the vague idea of it, and literature, its many innuendoes and fictive worlds, was the currency we shared, our medium of exchange. Yes, all that, and I could see her spirit was trying to heal.

So would I look at her poetry?

Yes, but the professor in me insisted: Thou Shalt Write Poetry. Because it will, somehow, –be good for you, though I don't really know how or why. I wanted her to be my literature student again, the 'A' student she had turned out to be in the upper division modern American lit class she had taken almost twenty years earlier. I wanted her engaged in the writing life, and it suddenly occurred to me that she could do something for me.

"Carole," I said, "I've been working on a novel now for almost ten years. I keep revising it. I need someone with a really good critical mind, and a poetic mind, to write a hard-nosed critique of the thing. I think you'd be perfect for the job."

"What's it called?" she asked.

"*Labors of Love*. But I don't like that title. If I send you a copy of the manuscript to your Stillwater address, will you scribble your comments all over it? You send me your poems, and I'll do the same for you."

"Yes," she smiled, "send me your novel. I'll do my best with it." In a few minutes she struggled up from her chair, whispered a farewell, and went away.

I was bewildered as I watched her walk away. Who was this gaunt ghost of her former self? What terrible damage had the bullets done to her, her spirit, and what madness had possessed the man who would want to destroy such a vulnerable human being? Yet she had survived, and there was a certain Hans in Stillwater taking care of her, and she was riding again. And there was poetry, perhaps deepened by the dark tones she suddenly had come to know by heart.

I resolved to do my little bit: stay in touch, encourage her, be her mentor too, and let her assert her authority over my words. In this way I maybe could help Carole on her difficult path to recovery.

Little did either of us suspect that the easy part of her journey was already done.

Carole sent a few poems by mail, and I returned to her my forthright suggestions for revision. I wanted her to sense that I was not holding back my criticism of her work—that I believed in her emotional and mental strength. When she returned my novel manuscript, it took me only a few moments to understand that I had underestimated her intellectual staying power. In a light but florid pencil hand she had provided marginal comments on most of the 400-page manuscript. It immediately became clear that I needed to take them seriously.

The novel whose title was a cliché, *Labors of Love*, had been pompously and ironically renamed *The Savior of America* when Carole received it from me. The story had been conceived in 1982, at a time when I had lost sight of Carole, and it had gone through two wholesale revisions in the next ten years. It was, in my mind, the story about the decline of a city neighborhood as seen through the eyes of its protagonist Sal (Salvatore: "Savior"), unemployed as he works to uncover the source of decline. His search, in my mind, was also a journey inward—to the religious "bottom of it all" signified by a grand cathedral with a compromised architectural design, and to the roots of his own emotional and sexual dissatisfaction. His anger and frustration, like that of others in the story, was often expressed in sexual terms at odds with his more benign sense of things. In the end peace-loving Sal, armed with a gun, plans to assassinate the old man he sees as the personification of the problems all around. But when he confronts the old man he is incapable of pulling the trigger.

On looking back now I see how stupidly insensitive I was to Carole's emotional condition—how my Doctor of Philosophy had taught me little about the kind of nurturing Carole was looking for. Carole's criticisms of my fictive labor of love made it clear that my Sal, my savior of America, was making some terrible mistakes on his journey toward self-understanding. In short, Carole made it very clear that my novel was going very wrong.

I discovered, in penciled handwriting so faint it seemed to be holding back out of shy kindness, how fine-tuned, discriminating, and sophisticated her intelligence and aesthetic sense are. Her comments could be appreciative and full of praise—"I love this page," "good sentence," "great last line!" "very nice writing," "good way to end a chapter." And she could insist on precision, the importance of detail: "I would say 'velour' fabric rather than velvet." "End the paragraph with 'He turned away.'" "Spelling 'T-shirt' might look nicer on the page." Or again: "I think it would be a different fabric, perhaps silk? Velvet is used mainly for evening gowns."

More importantly she was fine-tuned to what was atonal, false, and forced in my words: "Very childish thinking on Sal's part." "This is too simplistic and immature for me." "Something from a cheap novel." "I wish this scene would be more subtle and tasteful." "A little more subtle so it doesn't sound like a lecture." "This prose is a little flat." "This chapter needs a lot of work." "Dull beginning of this chapter." "Good sentence except for the repetition of 'away.'" "This seems a bit melodramatic." "This is phony to me."

She directed sharp criticism at my main character, Sal, not so much for his behaviors as against the language and fantasies that expressed his anger and frustration: "I don't feel much of Sal's love/respect for anyone." "Does he have to be so scornful in tone?" "Quite childish, don't you think?"

What most troubled Carole were the several connections between sex and violence. Sal, my protagonist, the main character I wanted readers to identify and sympathize with, she saw in a light that violated my intentions. She did not hold back: "Sal crosses the line between sex and violence very easily, it seems." "Again the latent violence." "This outburst of his seems quite overdone. It comes out of nowhere and seems to have more to do with violence rather than sex itself." "Sal seems to be in such a power struggle with women." "Again, an apparent over-reaction of anger to the actual situation. The latent violence in Sal. I'm not trying to tell you you should necessarily modify this scene, but I'm just trying to point out that he's the one with the problem." "Talk like this is really hard for me to take." "Sal seems like a destroyer of women's dreams." "What does this hatefulness toward women mean? Am I supposed to accept this for a fact? A given?"

And just once Carole had kind words for my hero Sal: "Finally! He is finally allowing himself some appropriate emotions."

Carole's criticisms were hard for me to live with. I was the professor, and she was the student. I had worked hard on the novel, and her comments seemed at odds with what I thought I was saying. Why didn't she see that Sal was a good guy, not a woman-hating jerk? I liked Sal, for all his flaws. He was, translated into a fiction, like me. If Carole's criticisms were valid, I'd have to confront the possibility that I was like Carole's Sal.

I didn't want to believe that. I read and reread Carole's comments to let their importance sink in. Then page by page I began to revise—that is, re-envision—what was implicit in my words. And page by page I did not merely touch it up; I rewrote it entirely. On October 10, 1993, I completed what I now call Carole's revision, one of several yet to come, of a much-improved novel that was beginning to satisfy me and live up to Carole's expectations of both me and Sal. Eventually it was published as *A Canticle for Bread and Stones*.

The trauma Carole experienced offered cynicism as a way of life, but she did not let her wounds destroy the generosity of spirit at the core of her identity. As a victim of violence Carole had good reason to be especially sensitive to innuendoes that appeared to approve of the brutality that wounded her. Raised as a Lutheran, she had to negotiate her way through the moral dilemmas posed by the Vietnam War and the sixties cultural revolution that swept into small-town Winona when she was still a high school girl. How would the anti-war crusaders, the romantic idealists, the feminists, and those experimenting with freer sexual mores affect her traditional Lutheran upbringing? Would she reject her traditional beliefs or creatively synthesize them with the new counter-cultural mores?

It is revealing, and perhaps indicative of the strength of her Christian convictions and compassion, that within weeks of her release from the Mayo Clinic she, with her parents, attended a memorial service for her late husband Jay at his burial site. She also began writing poems about him and reflecting on her life in a journal. Jay's attempt to murder her, his rage, and his suicide raised theological issues for her. How could God allow such things to happen, and how could belief in God be reconfigured in light of such evils? How could Jay have done what he did, and what happened to him after he took his own life?

She verbally expressed anger, but the anger was not seen in her non-verbal behaviors. Her heart could not cry out loud for revenge. She was profoundly sad, probably depressed, and grieved for him as she tried to heal herself. Her way to heal her emotional trauma was to understand Jay's life sympathetically.

When Carole moved into Hans' Helvetia Stables after the shooting, she began to move on with her life. Here she became close to a man who shared the love of her life, horses. And here one horse in particular—Shamu—captured Carole's heart. Like Carole, Shamu had been abused previously and had little reason to trust human beings. Little by little Shamu bonded with Carole as their mutual healing took hold.

On December 10, 1993, Carole married Hans Senn. I was happy for her and imagined that their lives would be much improved.

If Hans was the 44-year-old adult from Switzerland who sold Carole her first horse when she was fifteen years old, he was also master horseman who knew that to ride a horse beautifully required balance and trust and that a beautiful ride liberated the spirit from the world's gravity. Born and raised in Switzerland and other parts of Europe, Hans emigrated to the U.S. in 1962 and established himself in equestrian circles as a master of show jumping, dressage, eventing, and fox hunting. He himself rode in competitive events and became respected as a judge at shows and competitions. In 1990 he coordinated the equestrian events of the Olympic Festival. At Hans' Helvetia Stables in Stillwater, Carole entered a setting where mastery of horsemanship was an art practiced at a high level with discipline and grace.

Comments made in *Apropos Horses and Riders* (2006), a small book beautifully written and illustrated by Hans and venerated by expert contemporary equestrians, reveal much about the ideals that Hans represented. In her introduction to the book, Nell Krumhout says, "Aside from emerging as a brilliant book on the equine/human relationship, much of [Hans'] wisdom applies to human/human relationships, human Higher-Power relationships, and relationships with ourselves." She invites us to consider these lines written by Hans in the book: "Only constant training and the consequent synchronization of two minds and two beating hearts bring balance and harmony." "True communication is a revelation, not a contest." "If your expectations are low, you cannot excel."

I found other revelations in this beautiful book: "Balance is better than grip." "Your eye control makes your first commitment to go from here to there." "Agreement is only possible if you work at it." "When talking and listening occur, a conversation gains clarity and horse and rider begin to realize that they now occupy a common ground." "Never blame the horse for not understanding you; if necessary, you must simplify your language. The aids should be non-conflicting, simple, and consistent. They should be communicative, functional, proportional, and well-timed."

"I dedicate this book to my wife Carole," Hans says on the dedicatory page, and on page one he adds quite simply and gracefully, "She was a very beautiful and sensitive rider. Here is one of her poems":

> I hear silent shots
> ringing in memory like
> churchbells from childhood.

Now and then following her marriage to Hans, Carole sent me a few poems. They were remarkably good, and they were adding up. I suspected that writing them was also therapeutic, allowing her to see more deeply into what she had experienced and freeing her to express herself. Did they have healing power? Would they help her cope and recover? I wondered: In a culture where violence against women was routine and often kept from view, did Carole have an important story to tell not only to herself but to the world? Did she have a book in her?

Perhaps one by one she would be able to write enough really good poems to make a book of them. When I posed the question, she shied away from it, but in her silence I could hear her say it was an idea, like her new life with horses and Hans, she loved.

Meanwhile, quietly and privately, Carole began keeping a journal on November 6, 1994.

"A woman's voice keeps haunting me the last few days," is its first line. In her fine hand, Carole recorded some of her most intimate thoughts for the next three months, with entries suddenly coming to an end on January 12, 1995.

My phone rang about nine p.m. on March 19, 1995, and I was surprised to hear the voice of Carole's brother Tom on the other end. The profound bad news had a flatness to it: Carole had suffered a brain aneurysm and was in a coma on life-support at the Stillwater Medical Center. No, she was not expected to live. And no, the aneurysm was not related to her gunshot wounds. It was a terrible, terrible stroke of bad luck.

I said farewell to her when I turned off the light and went to bed that night.

Carole, I learned, had suffered what is technically called a subarachnoid hemorrhage, bleeding from a ruptured cerebral aneurysm, a weakness in the wall of a brain artery. The rupture, a form of what is also commonly called a stroke, is usually preceded by a "thunderclap headache" that leads to vomiting, confusion and loss of consciousness. Carole's was the most severe type, one that sends victims into a coma. Such hemorrhages occur in 9.1 out of 100,000 people annually, a tiny percentage of the general population. Only ten percent survive, and those who do suffer major physical and cognitive impairment. She was experiencing paralysis, notably in her dominant right (writing) hand, and muscular rigidity all over her body. She would never walk again unaided, if she ever woke up.

Her brother Tom left me with little hope that she would survive, and I fell into despair thinking about the permanent damage done to her wonderful mind. For the next few days I waited for the phone to ring, and when I tried to call her brother Tom, I got no response. Carole's parents, her brothers and sister were holding vigils, waiting. I waited too, not knowing if the worst would be her living or dying.

Carole's new journey began with her immediate transfer from the Stillwater hospital to the St. Paul-Ramsey Medical Center. There she underwent a left frontal craniotomy, which required surgery to relieve the brain of blood and to address the aneurysm flaw. From there she was transferred to Bethesda Lutheran Hospital for respiratory and tracheotomy care, and then to St. Joseph's Hospital, where she was treated for brain seizure activity. From St. Joseph's, she was sent back to Bethesda. In all she spent almost four months in hospitals, most of the time on life-support. The official Bethesda report described her as a "spastic quadriplegic in a vegetative state with a feeding tube." Her movement out of a coma was gradual, and progress was slow until the final two weeks when she began to show signs of regaining consciousness.

Expert medical procedures no doubt saved her life, but the slow return to consciousness had much to do with family and friends. Carole's father and mother were constantly at her side, and there were many visits from Helen, Jim, Tom and Christine. Her husband Hans and many friends were frequent visitors. As Carole slept on and on they spoke out loud to her, read whole chapters of books, helped her pet her dog, rubbed lotion on her arms, brought in items carrying scents from the barn, and played music, Mozart, for her. A coma stimulation program designed to determine if her responses were reflexive or deliberate was put in place. Her responses were monitored, as were her facial expressions. Friends watched for small movements stimulated by the honking of horns, by air being blown on her face, by her name being called, by the music, or by pictures of loved ones and horses being shown to her. A few positive signs began appearing a month after the aneurysm occurred. In slow time she began blinking her eyes, smiling, laughing, crying, nodding her head in response to questions, grunting, groping out with a hand to touch someone. Then her eyes began to scan the photos in a picture book, pausing when she got to pictures of herself with Hans and her favorite horse Shamu.

Who knows if and how her body registered the words, feelings, and sensations her friends and family sent her way? Who knows if words read out loud in her hospital room in some indecipherable way impressed themselves on a mind cognitively impaired but still numinous with life? Did she, like a ghost imprisoned in a house, hear people outside her door calling for her, refusing to believe there was nobody home?

When she was discharged from Bethesda on July 24, 1995, and placed in long-term residential care in White Bear Care Center, she was fully awake and had a tracheostomy and feeding tube still in place.

Carole was alive. The beautiful young woman was disfigured and confined to a bed and wheelchair from paralysis and muscle rigidity. She was suffering from aphasia and motor speech disorders that affected all areas of communication, expressive and receptive language, sound production, reading and writing. The medical reports made it clear that she would never ride a horse again and was doomed to be "cognitively impaired."

What are the odds, we ask ourselves, that such misfortunes should strike the same person so violently not once but twice? And so "unfair," as if the terrible violence that targeted her was the expression of a malign evil deeply woven into the fabric of existence.

As a professor of literature, I looked to books for explanations for such mysteries, just as I had hoped Carole would find explanations and consolation in the poems she was writing until the aneurysm occurred. The hope for the birth of that book of poems about the mind healing itself from the damage done by verbal abuse, bullets, and a pickup truck faded in my mind. Carole seemed like someone else. When I visited her at Ramsey Hospital, she did not seem aware of my existence in the room. If she woke up she might be able to make sounds, but would she ever be able to make words? Her fingers were twisted. She would not be able to write.

What a loss, I told myself again and again, unaware that anything positive could be gained.

The aneurysm came as a shock to Carole's family and friends, and to her husband Hans. What could they do for a person in a coma, hooked up to a maze of life-support devices? To avoid confronting the pain of her situation my impulse was to stay away, until she passed away. I visited her at the St Paul-Ramsey Medical Center twice and did a lot of talking to what seemed myself in her hospital room. At St. Joseph's Hospital, the nurse I talked to weeks later made it clear that Carole was not improving. She kept having seizures, the nurse said, and without actually saying it the nurse offered little hope.

The commitment of Carole's parents, family members, and friends to her survival is incalculable, and the distances they traveled to spend hours with her were considerable. Friends and family came often to offer her their presence, small gifts, and words, even when week after week their presence, small gifts, and words fell on what seemed like deaf ears. Family members and Hans, of course, were often at her side. But there were serious medical and financial issues to face as Carole slowly began waking up. Hans' devotion was profound, and his commitment to the oath he took—"In sickness and health, 'til death do us part"—he lived up to in word and deed. But he too needed help.

Carole's father Arnold died in August 1996, a year and a half after the aneurysm. He and Carole's mother Merle had spent most of that time at her side. "We all think that it took the life right out of him," said Carole's brother Tom.

When Carole was admitted into the long-term care facilities in White Bear Lake and Golden Valley Courage Center she entered what perhaps was the most difficult phase of her harrowing journey. Her progress toward consciousness was painfully slow and uneven, and her disabilities perhaps too severe for the services the center could offer. My wife Monica and I visited her several times at the White Bear Lake facility, and later at the Courage Center. During these visits she was heavily medicated and could not walk or speak, responding to questions with gestures, facial expressions, laughter and grunts. The laughter seemed out of place. She had gained a lot of weight, and though nurses, especially in the White Bear Lake facility, were kind and caring to her, she spent many hours alone.

Eventually Carole began using a notepad and pencil to communicate her needs. She could not use her left thumb and could not turn the pages of her notepad. She tried to speak, and began to make single-word scrawls with her left hand.

There were chilling times. I recall hearing strange howls in the Courage Center facility as I walked toward her room to visit her. The howls were deep, full of sorrow. Carole, alone in her room, expressing the depth of her depression.

But during these visits she managed laughter too, some of it raucous, full-bodied. What gradually became apparent over the course of my visits to the nursing homes was that she was not merely awake and increasingly awake, but also sharp. She seemed to understand what was said to her, responding at first with a slow nod of the head, then with her face and eyes. To fill in some of the silences, I resorted to bad humor, and she laughed. I made bad puns, and she laughed. I made up some bad rhymes, and she laughed. I told long jokes, and she laughed. I wondered whether she really "got" the jokes—was her laughter in some sense an "automatic" response? So I tried complex jokes on her, just to see—and she laughed and howled at the right times and lines. She definitely "got" them.

Carole was completely dependent on others for all activities of daily living. She was officially "cognitively impaired," but seemed very much at home, upstairs.

As a student of literature, I had good reason to marvel at the human mind's capacity to invent, shape, and create meaning from words touched in some way by intensely felt experiences. I did so without ever understanding what I meant by the word "mind," and with little scientific knowledge of the human brain's ways and capacities. Carole, before her misfortunes, was clearly a highly intelligent, if habitually quiet, young woman. If the shooting deepened her silence, did the aneurysm destroy her mind? Was her coma a long sleep necessary to her body's recovery and was it simultaneously like a monk's meditative retreat required if her mind was to be reborn? Could a severely damaged brain heal itself and restore a mind? Could a mind, encouraged by the loving presence of family and friends in hospital and nursing home rooms, restore a brain?

I do not know what scientists have to say about questions like this, and the progress I saw in Carole was less obviously steady than it was painful. But it became increasingly evident that she speechlessly understood what was said to her and had opinions of her own, one in particular. She was not shy about letting it be known that life in the Courage Center was not for her.

After their marriage, she and Hans had been constructing a new home for themselves, but they spent only one night together in it before the aneurysm struck. The new home was not handicap accessible, and this posed problems for Carole's ongoing care. Help came to Hans by way of Cindy Hanson and Nan Cowin. Before the stroke, Cindy and Nan were boarders at Hans' farm and had come to know Carole through their mutual interests in horses. After the aneurysm, they visited Carole in the hospital and then began helping Hans negotiate the difficulties posed by medical decisions, costs, insurance, and therapy options. They eventually became trustees and guardians after Hans set up a trust on Carole's behalf.

Others stepped in to help. Carol Hop, a neighbor of Hans, knew Carole as the woman riding horses when she dropped by on two separate occasions to bring Christmas cookies. But a strange feeling stayed with Carol Hop after the two brief encounters. She did not understand the feeling but sensed that this neighbor-stranger would someday become important to her. As a religious person she wondered if God was speaking to her, and after visiting her in the hospital, she could not get Carole out of her mind. She prayed.

Onlookers were astonished when Carole, during one of Carol Hop's visits, spoke some of her first understandable words. "I would like that," she said when Carol Hop asked if she wanted more visits. Carol Hop's visits to the White Bear Lake and Courage Center nursing homes became routine, and God's calling became clear. She took it upon herself to lessen Hans' burden and take Carole on in foster care. She sold her home but kept a portion of the acreage, and with the assistance of Hans, she built a handicap-accessible duplex on the back acres of what once was the Helvetia Stables. After four years of living in hospitals and nursing homes, Carole moved into the Hop residence on April 12, 1999. There Carol Hop and Carole lived in one half of the house, and Carol Hop's daughter Jody, and Jody's paraplegic husband, lived in the other half. In her new home, Carole was slowly weaned off many of her medications and introduced to solid foods. Here Hans, and Wayne Wood, a stable hand at Helvetia, visited her frequently and took her out on excursions in their cars. Here, within view of the horses Carole loved, Carole had a room of her own and received the loving care of a devoted husband and friends.

"She [Carol Hop] is an angel," wrote Carole in 2014.

From the Hop residence Carole's road to rehabilitation took new turns. She began regular swimming activities and exercises to improve muscle flexion. Hans took her nearly every week to the Stillwater Courage Center for swimming and hydro-therapy, assisted by volunteers at the Center. With the aid of others she tried to walk with a walker. At the Courage Center, she had refused to use a Dynavox communication system, and later she became discouraged with speech therapy sessions. Then, in June of 2006, Carole had a change of heart and began working with Anne Gerber, a speech therapist, at Carole's Stillwater home.

Meanwhile, Hans remained loyal to her. To travel with Carole required the strength to lift Carole and her wheelchair into his car. He was a small man, about five-feet-five, but he was strong. He brought Carole to visit family and friends in Winona, once to the nursing home where Carole's mother was spending her last days. On another visit, Carole was reunited with her friend Margaret Tweedy, herself afflicted by crippling rheumatoid arthritis. The two of them sat close to each other, sharp as ever, both of them given to outbursts of laughter. As I watched 84-year-old Hans, "an existentialist" (Carole's words), maneuvering Carole into his car for the long ride back home to Stillwater, I began believing again in saints.

But not in miracles. Hans, and Carole's family and friends, put in many long hours of hard work to help her survive.

Following months of illness, Hans died on November 10, 2010.

Then one day Carole expressed to Anne a desire to write a memoir, and before long, Carole began writing poems again.

In *The Golden Bough*, Sir James Frazer's classic study of pre-Christian societies, he describes strange practices that caught my attention while Carole was, as she often was, out of sight and out of mind. To ward off "evils"—diseases, insanities and violence in their various forms—so-called "primitive" peoples routinely "transferred" the evils to objects, aspects of nature, or other people. On the island of Rock near New Guinea, for example, Frazer noticed that natives would gather to scream, curse, howl, and beat the air with sticks in order to scare troubles away from their villages. In other societies, ills would be projected onto an animal, effigy, or object like a pumpkin, or small boats were stocked with rice and eggs and sent floating downstream toward evil powers waiting for them as villagers remained on shore praying for the powers to free them from smallpox, plagues, and other afflictions. Humans often were the vehicles for transferring ills—a masked priest, for example, taking it upon himself to conjure a disease out of a sick person into himself, the priest then shamming the death of his own body so the disease would depart, leaving the priest and the sick person behind, presumably reborn and whole.

Today we call such rituals, so lacking in scientific basis, superstitious.

Yet in the "civilized" Western world certain similar practices persist. The Judeo-Christian tradition still honors Passover. This ritual is based on the practice of slaughtering a spring lamb and using its blood to mark the doors of those who want God to spare their first-born from death. As part of the City Dionysia, the drama festival held annually in ancient Greek cities, a goat (or *tragados*) was ritually slaughtered as a sacrifice. From *tragados* we derive our word "tragedy." In the Christian tradition, the Christ figure himself is a "scapegoat," an innocent who takes upon himself all of mankind's sins so individuals who believe in the sacrifice may be redeemed. In these rituals, and in many of those practiced in non-Western "primitive" societies, an innocent—a lamb, a goat, an actual human being—is sacrificed for the greater good of the community.

Carole has not been deliberately sacrificed; her misfortunes have resulted from what we could call unfortunate circumstances and chance, rather than ritual. But it is difficult not to associate her example with the way a tragedy may redeem communities by bringing people together in new ways.

What value does Carole's life have for us, whether we believe in the gods or a God or heaven or not? We can measure this value in terms of how her family, friends, and even acquaintances responded to her suffering. Her parents, her brothers and sisters, her other relatives and friends have been moved, and transformed, by her exceptional example.

Friends who read books to the silent walls in her hospital and nursing home rooms, who avoided her out of inability to confront her suffering yet were with her in thought and prayer, were transformed, bonded into a better and more profoundly sympathetic understanding of the Preacher's wisdom—that time and chance happeneth to us all, that here but for fortune go I. Above all Hans, the "existentialist," who loved her to the end, realized his best humanity and provided us an example of how to accept the transfer of Carole's troubles to himself.

Carole's story is no "American" success story. She did not lift herself to success by herself. Nor is it a story about miraculous divine intervention. Carole has survived horrifying events, and her suffering is ongoing.

She endures pain, loneliness, confusion, and helplessness day by day. In her wheelchair and bed she lives with dreams of flying away on Shamu's back. And hers is an incompletely told story if we imagine that Carole has not required enormous personal sacrifices of family members and friends. But the happy note in Carole's life is that she has moved those who know her, that their compassion has resonated into the larger community, and that she wants to give us a memoir so this movement may live on.

Like Churchbells from Childhood

*Carole's Memoir 2010–2012
and Poems 1992–1993*

Prairie Breeze

When I was 24 years old, I met a man while I was riding at the Ridge View stable. Sabon was the brother of the stable's farrier. Although I do not remember the details of our meeting we soon became boyfriend and girlfriend. I shared with him my interest, which was to raise Nubian goats and he shared with me his interest in guitar playing. Together we decided to build a log cabin in the small town of Viroqua, which was outside of La Crosse, Wisconsin. After the log cabin was built Sabon and I were married at his parents' country home in La Crosse. We then began our journey with raising and milking Nubian goats. I became unsatisfied in the marriage after two years, and Sabon and I parted ways. When I look back on my life with Sabon, I realize that it was physically hard farming and even harder living in isolation.

Then I met Jay.

We lived in the rural parts of Iowa, surrounded by hills and valleys, corn fields and hay. Prairie Breeze was the name of our fourteen-horse stable where we boarded horses. Our home, a white, two-story farm house with a front porch, was owned by my mother-in-law, Marge. My husband of three years, Jay, was a quiet man. He had harsh words that broke my character down when he was angry. He had a mental disorder that was not diagnosed but could be felt.

Marge, Jay's mother, also lived with us. She was a drinker who couldn't drive. She had a nasty temper but also was sweet. Marge was visited weekly by a hairdresser who would come to our home to color her hair blonde and set her perms in our kitchen.

I was in an unhappy marriage. I was a listener and internalized my pain. The only thing that relieved my world of hurt was horses and riding.

My opportunity to escape from Jay's world began in the summer. My interest in Hans Senn's show jumping and dressage method, and his philosophies landed me in Stillwater, Minnesota at his stable, Helvetia. Hans, a native of Switzerland, gave me an opportunity to learn his riding style by letting me assist in the training of his horses. I was paid for my work and also provided with a place to stay. Jay did not like my new work. This escape to Hans' was a relief from stress and abuse at home.

It was during a visit home for Thanksgiving in 1986 when my old life ended and my new life began. It was 4:30 in the afternoon when I walked into Marge getting her hair done by the aide in the kitchen.

"Hi there," Marge said.

"Hello," I responded.

In walked Jay, and we exchanged greetings. Jay left the room to get his briefcase that contained the papers on the race horses that were boarded at Prairie Breeze. When he returned from the bedroom Jay said, "We need to talk," as he headed out the front door toward the pickup truck with his briefcase in hand.

I simply replied, "O.K." and willingly followed him, all the while my mind pondering what we might be discussing regarding the horses.

We left in his truck with the briefcase between us, but I questioned to myself why he had it. He took the truck out into the cornfields. He was talking about his anger with me being gone. He fumbled in the case and pulled out a gun. My first reaction was not fear, just wonderment at what he was doing. I quickly learned that the gun was for me as he pointed it my way. I said, "No! No! No!" Despite my pleas, he began shooting. First at my heart, followed by my left forearm and left elbow, with the final shot to the back of my head at my neck and the base of my spine. Seven or eight bullets entered me with a warm sensation. I then had a vision during the shooting that I was in Heaven and saw the Son, Father and Holy Ghost in bodily form. Heaven then quickly vanished and the reality of the situation lay before me. I escaped from the stopped truck. I began running, running in the cornfields to the highway.

Marge, having sensed something was not right when we left, called an ambulance. The ambulance was arriving as I too was running to the house on the highway. Meanwhile, Jay drove back to the farm house, parked next to it and shot himself with one bullet. He died on the way to the hospital. I was taken by ambulance to the Decorah hospital and then sent on to Mayo by helicopter.

My memory of the ambulance ride and then the helicopter ride is one of "remembering," beyond words.

To My Husband

In the stillness of summer
I saw you grasping,
Tearing the rosebushes
Out of their white bed of stones,
Blood charging through their arteries,
Upended champagne glass roots
Stiffened into shock.

1992

Seized by Terror

Seized by terror,
He would run away from me
Like a panicky horse,
He'd wake in some quiet of darkness
Never sleeping
More than a couple of hours.
I might wake in the night, too,
In my sleep missing
His breathing, waking
Only to see the bright, crazed
Headlights of his truck reaching in
To sweep around the floral papered walls
Of our farmhouse.

Then he was gone, and
I would lie there
In the empty garden, our bed,
Listening to the roaring and bouncing
Of semi-trucks and trailers
Over the rough concrete highway.
It was then that some deep,
Wordless part of me knew
He would always be leaving.

1992

Santos

When I found him he was ruined,
His rider a punishing weight,
all the more frightening
for being inescapable.
Now it is my turn
to sit on his rigid back
and he tosses his head wildly.

Nervous sweat dampens
the arch of his seal brown neck.
It's his language of perfect memory
and I try to listen without error,
for this, too, is my salvation.

I whisper to him
with the softness of my hands
on the reins, my prayer:

Santos, from our rides through time,
from our partnership allow
a loosening of knots of pain
and a constant way of finding
my own strengthening rhythm
and your joyfulness, your playful gaits.

February 26, 1992

Color Wheel

My visual and tactical experiences began after the shooting, remained throughout my recovery, and are currently still present. The description of my experience is as if describing another sense, "a sixth sense." The best verbal depiction to get one to come close to the experiences I have is for one to imagine color, of the mind's eye. This occurs when my eyes are shut and during my dreams. A kaleidoscope of color is continuously moving but captured in form. The color wheel has depth, texture and movement—of brown velvet drapes with silk ribbon tied at the top flowing freely downward. One day after the shooting I was visited at the hospital by a close group of family and friends who all played a role in my recovery. The color wheel allowed me to see all of them in a new perspective. It was the same people I had known, some of them over a lifetime; however, my mind's eye was capturing them in a new light.

With the many visitors that came to see me, my image of them was captured in color: burgundy for Mom and my brother Tom, cobalt blue for Dad, moon blue for my brother Jim, yellow for my sister Helen, forest green for my friend Hans, and light brown, olive green and orange for my friend Orval. Throughout their visits their concern for my health was apparent. They frequently expressed their concerns and I always responded by saying, "I'm alive," just like I said in the helicopter to the male nurse that was taking care of me.

Orval, our neighbor, was a farmer who lived down the road from Prairie Breeze, the home and stable where my husband Jay grew up. I had met Orval soon after my marriage and we developed a close friendship. We shared similar passions: horses, farming and good conversation, and I shouldn't forget our talks about the "weather." Orval farmed corn and hay, which he sold in small and large bales. He supplied us with the hay to feed our horses at Prairie Breeze. Orval's visits to me in the hospital brought comfort and the good memories of Prairie Breeze.

On one of Orval's visits he said he had gone to the field the next day after my shooting. He had seen my blood and stated how it was like I was a deer shot in the field and left to die. I heard his anxious words and my mind's eye spun the image into a kaleidoscope of red, burgundy, and purple in which I sat observing.

My mother and father made the half-hour drive from Winona to the Mayo Clinic to visit me. I remember little of the details of their visits, but I do remember that when my mother came she did what mothers do, she brushed my hair and talked to me. My mother was one who under pressure was very anxious. She talked a lot and kept herself busy. As a child, I knew her level of anxiousness by the amount of freshly baked cookies waiting for me when I came through the door, or if she was on the phone with one of her girlfriends, Bonnie, Helen, or Jean.

My father, on the other hand, quietly sat by my side during his visits or read the paper out loud. Despite his quiet demeanor, my father's soul could be felt when you were in his presence. His moves were graceful yet solid. His peach skin and soft eyes held a sense of comfort that all was going to be alright. Upon reflection, maybe this is why I went to him with my life's problems. He listened, he supported me, and through that I felt guided. My love for horses was shared with my father. Although he did not ride, he was inspired by my passion. He supported my riding career with encouragement and love.

My brother Tom, who fell third in line of the Stoa children, was an intern ER doctor in Pennsylvania at the time of the shooting. I felt reassured knowing that he was speaking to my doctors at Mayo about my recovery. He and his wife Christine have two children, Ryan and John.

Jim is the second oldest and has a very humble and caring heart. He has five children: Patrick, Craig, Jennifer, Jim, and Chris. Jim's presence in the hospital room brought peace. Jim became a fifth-grade teacher straight out of college. He later became manager, alongside our father Arnold, of the Country Kitchen in Janesville, Wisconsin, formerly owned by our sister Helen and Robert. Jim lives with his life partner Gail, and together they have raised a blended family of seven children.

Helen is the oldest child. With her the oldest and I the youngest, I as a child looked up to her. She was named Miss Winona and I can still remember her riding that float in the Steamboat Days parade. When I was in sixth grade Helen gave me a blue parakeet for a Christmas gift. To this day, I still look at parakeet books and secretly wish I had a new one.

Helen went to college at Northwestern University in Illinois. She left Illinois to move to New York to embark on a modeling career. She met her husband, Robert, in Chicago when she returned from New York. After her modeling career ended she became co-owner of Country Kitchen in Janesville, Wisconsin, which she later sold to our father Arnold. Helen and Robert had two boys and one boy from Helen's first marriage. Their names were Jim, Matt, and Dan.

Hans was the owner of Helvetia Stables, and I was one of the riders that worked his horses while learning his methods. I was touched by Hans' friendship. Shortly after the shooting, he visited me in the hospital and brought with him a giant teddy bear that made me laugh. The teddy bear stayed with me during my stay in the hospital.

As laughable as it may seem, Bing Crosby kept me company in my hospital room. It was the hardest point in my life and Bing contributed to my happiness and will to continue to live. His comedy melted away my pain and brought me to a place where I experienced joy and laughter. The remarks that brought me to tears were when Bing tried

Carole (center), her sister Helen, brothers Jim and Tom, and her parents

defying the aging process by saying, "You hit the 50s, then the 60s and then it's back to 39."

I am not sure if there were other "out of body" experiences I had. However, the one I do remember consists of me fast asleep softly snoring as my whole family stood next to me having casual conversation. From deep inside my sleep I observed this scene with much laughter.

I moved in with my parents for two months after leaving the hospital, after which I returned to my riding at Hans' stables, and soon thereafter was invited to move in with him. I accepted his offer and viewed him as my protector and soon my love. I lived with him for six years and then he asked me to be his wife. During these six years, I was allowed the safety and protection I needed to heal my body, mind, and spirit from my terrible shooting tragedy. Two years into my healing Jay came to me in a dream. In the dream, Jay was bringing children's books to the poor children in the urban areas of Chicago. There was a knowing sense in the dream that he was an angel helping these children. When I woke, I had peace in my heart about everything that took place that dreadful day of the shooting. I felt released from my pain and the words "I'm alive" took on a whole new meaning. I had hope and will again.

Sun Chimes

The sun lifts up above green hills,
assumes its monarchy over dewy morning.
The ancient cultivator pulled by a mule
makes incisions with curved tines in the soil.
The uncertain tread of my footsteps follows.
Shadows rustle between rows of corn.
Afternoon brings a numbness to my hands.
We come to rest at the end of a furrow.
The mule stands quietly in his traces,
shaking his head to loosen the reins,
Stretching his neck down,
hoping for a bite of grass.

Chimes of light play all around us
in grasses and tall weeds.
Soon again the sun, evanescent lover,
with softest kisses will begin to leave me
in a darkening lowland.

March 1993

The Sun, the Moon and the Thunderstorm

The following people mentioned in this chapter were pivotal people that deeply changed my outlook and perspective on life. They gifted me with the knowledge of the world, as they knew it. In my mind I saw the world in symbolic lights.

Jesus Christ is the sun, Moses is the moon, and Mohammed is the thunderstorm. Many people idolize Jesus Christ without truly understanding him. Which makes me sad. I began to see Christ more clearly after my injury. His life was an example of a willingness to live, just as I made the choice for survival in the truck the day of my shooting. Many people live daily idolizing Jesus Christ without a willingness for life. I question if it takes suffering to reach this depth of understanding. Christ is our leader guiding us in how we should walk through life. When we fall we should pick ourselves up and walk. When we meet up with the evil of this earth we must meet it with forgiveness and release its hold. What better of a teacher than Jesus Christ?

The Holy Ghost is represented in the wind and jet stream. It is all encompassing, the pulse of life. At times its presence is very subtle, whereas other moments it is fierce. Many people separate themselves from the Holy Ghost not aware that it is the very breath we breath.

Moses is seen in the cycles of the moon and represents the Ten Commandments, the foundation we live by. The full moon is our perfect self. In the phases of the moon we are given multiple chances to start anew. As the moon waxes, our life force is pulling our essence from our being. The crescent moon to the half-moon inches us forward, unveiling our true nature. When the moon is full it is time to live in the moment, letting our wholeness, our divine nature shine. Our people have fallen from the natural rhythms of the moon. We live by discord versus harmony.

Mohammad's scriptures are like bolts of lightning and crashes of thunder. The lightning demands our attention to look within. A thunderstorm forces us to be present. The clouds are angels reminding us of God's guiding presence.

As I moved through my younger life trying to make sense of my inner spirit I now can see the people that helped guide me to find myself.

Emilio was my mentor. After the shooting my mind's eye spun him into a color of jade green, maybe because of the color of his eyes. I met him when I was 20 years old; he was my American Literature professor at Winona State University. He changed my perception of how I viewed literature and my world expanded from gym, swimming, and horses to the world of stories and poems. In his classroom I felt like a miner in a windowless cave searching for gold and silver. I was exhilarated by entering an unknown territory in the dark and searching for truth. I remember being inspired by the work of Ralph Waldo Emerson, Emily Dickinson, Henry David Thoreau, and Nathaniel Hawthorne's *Scarlet Letter*.

Emilio and I developed a close friendship. I later gave him editorial comments on one of his books, *A Canticle of Bread and Stone*. I was excited to be asked and did not realize the challenge I was in for. It helped me further develop my ability to critically analyze the written word.

Death Spiral

In the night of onyx,
slipping into slumber alone
with a brocade of thoughts,
a luxurious spiraling before
dissolving consciousness
is given the task
of finding you in dreams.

You have weight
in this snowy meadow.
Our skater's blades
spray ice sparks
as we diminish the circle
and join, stretching out our arms,
clasping hands to wrists.

You pull me around and round
your body in a backbend.

A wisp of my hair
falls loose, brushes the cruel,
ever wakeful sea.

February 22, 1993

Dressage

My favorite type of performance riding was dressage. You would ride in the ring solo, being judged on a set of patterns that are unique to the individual rider and horse. During your ride you were required to trot, canter, walk, and end with a trot. While I rode the musical works of Vivaldi, Handel, Bach, and Telemann played in my head. The composers of the Baroque era focused me and the rhythmic nature of the music moved beautifully with a canter. I can see now that my interest in dressage went beyond the sport. It represented life to me. The patterns in the ring mimicked the patterns in life and the classical music helped me give in to the moment. Every day is like a trot, situations rising and falling and the only balance you find is what you create. The canter is the special moments of life, moments of exhilaration and freedom. These moments are fleeting, ones to be present in, before they are gone.

I learned dressage riding from Hans the summer before my shooting. At this time I did not realize the future relationship I would have with Hans. I entered in my relationship with him purely from a standpoint of wanting to learn dressage. It was in 1993 that Hans and I married.

Hans' love allowed me to experience a different side of love than I had known, one that began from tragedy both in my life and his. We came together out of the need for survival and the loss of innocence. Our love was not first love, all passion and innocence, but a love of depth that captured broken pieces of our lives and character. Hans lost his first love and girlfriend in a motor vehicle accident in Switzerland when his brother was behind the wheel. And I had survived being shot by my husband. It was a love of harmony, but one that played a different song. A love that lasted sixteen years of marriage where we stood by each other surrounded in safety, giving each other space to heal and trust again.

Shamu was my wedding gift from Hans. He was a brown thoroughbred that stood seventeen hands high. We shared similar backgrounds of abuse. He was kind despite being named after a killer whale. He was a survivor too and maybe that's where the name came from. Shamu did not trust just any rider. I would like to think he could sense my salvation because I could sense his.

My good friend Orval—whom I met while married to my second husband, Jay—sold hay to our farm. I introduced him to Hans the summer I trained with Hans. Hans and Orval began a working relationship and Hans began buying hay from Orval. Orval was a deep friend of mine who listened to me as we talked about farming, weather, and horses. This was important to me at this time of my life because my husband Jay did not listen to me. Jay often ignored my words leaving me feeling horribly lonely. Orval stood by my side through my shooting and during my recovery. He would make me laugh and smile.

This is one of the reasons it was so tragic when he died of a farming accident involving a large bale machine on July 7, 1989.

Smooth Sailing

Looking beyond the fence
with a good eye
for a distance,
galloping
the last stride
stretching his neck downwards,
a pendulum,
hind legs brought underneath,
a gathering into flight
legs tucked up neatly
under the smooth arc of body.

March 1993

Carole on Dacell

Coma: The Nina, the Pinta, and the Santa Maria

Being in a coma was a journey. I set sail on a voyage that took place on the Mississippi as I was transferred from hospital to hospital. I was also released from the physical world to journey the spiritual realm within. While in a coma I had experiences that one might describe as a dream; however, they appeared to me more like perceptions of reality.

One of the perceptions I was in involved a love encounter with Orval, a dear friend. The scene while in the coma was warm and windy during the afternoon outside near a river. The sun was reflecting sharp like knives, off the water sending glistening rays of light to the surrounding area. I was with Orval making love. We were panting and it was pleasurable. Orval said, "I love you" and I immediately said, "I love you, too, Orval Harris." I still can remember the sensation of longing and the encompassing love that I felt engulfed in.

As I was transferred between three hospitals, I had perceptions of each one. The hospitals were ships. The *Nina* was my time when I was at Ramsey Hospital (now Regions Hospital). The *Pinta* was my time at Bethel, and the *Santa Maria* was at St. John's Hospital. The setting was always a dark evening and accompanying me were old wrinkly people and an ill child about eight years old. The ships were filled with hospital beds with all of us lying in them. I felt scared because people around me were dying but I wasn't. We transferred ships and all I remember was the dying were left behind as I was moved to the next ship. Once I entered the ship it was the same feeling and scene over again.

My Mother and Poetry

My mother had given me
a seashell when I was young.
The once animal had whorls
and spires on its creamy shell,
the interior smooth,
pink as the throat
of an azalea blossom.
It looked like an ear slashed from a slain god,
it was a gentle trumpet
giving sound to the
rhythm of waves.
Within my mother's pearly gift
sprang the cry of the ocean,
my ceaseless longing.

March 11, 1992

The Recovery

My road to recovery has been more than two decades and still continues. I went into a coma March 19, 1995, and it is currently 2015. What has propelled me forward in my recovery are the comforts and symbolism found in nature and my body's healing process that moves me from unconscious to conscious states.

My means to cope and inspiration are bird watching from the view out the French doors of my present Stillwater residence. The birds are like people to me. I observe their busyness. Each bird holds special meaning. The cardinals in their redness remind me of priests, both men and women. Gold finches are the pilots; they are good at navigating through the air. When I see them they take me to a place of freedom. Purple finches are astronauts that represent navigating the heavens. The lawyers of the sky are sparrows, which is evident by their plainness. The pileated woodpeckers are the architects forming design out of suet and tree trunks. The downy woodpecker is the construction worker. The hairy woodpecker is the hair dresser, because of its name. The rose grosbeaks, who are fancy in their coloring and carry themselves with importance, are the movie stars, the Robert Redfords and Meryl Streeps of the bird world. The nuthatches are the knitters and potters. The chickadees are the bankers, the CEOs, and the housewives. The house and winter wrens are the schoolteachers. The blue jay is the president. The bluebirds are the teenagers.

I moved to White Bear Lake Care Center in 1995 after I was stabilized. I could not talk. My meals and medication were primarily given to me through a feeding tube. The food I did get was pureed and was awful. The fluorescent lights gave me migraine headaches. I couldn't even look out my windows to see beauty. The houses around the care center were ugly. I was at the nursing home for three years. It was during my time there that I remembered Orval had died during the time between the shooting and my brain aneurysm. I also began to remember that I had a brain aneurysm. My memory of this space I was in—it was as if I'd been pulled from a conscious plane not allowing me to make sense of life events. Despite the pain of the conscious state of having had a brain aneurysm and realizing my close friend had died, I was happy to be gaining enough energy for coherent thoughts. I can remember jostling between the spiritual world and the physical plane of existence. Orval would come to visit me as an angel from the spiritual world. As I became more conscious I mourned his death and the death of my 'self' as I had known it. What kept me going was knowing that I was tough, which I learned from horses. I loved the old people that I was surrounded with and the space they created by being near the end of their lives. It's a space of wisdom, peace, and suffering. The nurses and aides that assisted my care offered me the gift of understanding compassion.

"Golden Valley"

My faith came from my roots in the Lutheran Church. My belief in Heaven and Christ as my Savior. I had already witnessed Heaven during the shooting and in a coma. It was no longer a concept; it was truth. I saw angels, my dear friend, Orval, by my side letting me know I was not alone. The spirit came in the form that I would recognize, my dear friend Orval. My experience at the Courage Center, Golden Valley, was yet another obstacle to test my faith. The loneliness, being mistreated, not being heard or seen. I was a product of what they wanted, not what I wanted.

I had a very difficult time in the Courage Center. My body was naturally resisting, sometimes to the breaking point. A broken wrist took six weeks to heal. I only went in the pool six times in six months. I equate it to watching the freedom die in a horse that has been cooped up in a stall and not set to pasture. The fluorescent lights on the ceiling in my bedroom hurt me. They hurt my eyes and gave me a headache. There was no possibility for healing or rest when I had lights on me that scrambled my energy. The mean aide would turn my lights on at 9:00 p.m. I would scream and no aide would come. Trapped. I could not walk or talk.

Hans was an existentialist. He was a good man. He was my coach, my guardian, my husband. He saw what my spirit needed, which was to leave the Courage Center, even though I didn't have words to express it at the time. He is in Heaven now with his red hair riding horses. It is in my dreams that we visit. He continues his coaching. I just had to change my ways of receiving it after his passing, in the symbols, in the dreams.

Since writing the memoir, I dreamt that I was riding horses. I also was the horse. My soul being one with a horse. The horse was Shamu. Shamu was a thoroughbred horse I trained that had been abused. I had been working with him prior to my aneurysm. I saw parallels in myself with Shamu's reluctance to trust and open up to the rider. There was rhythm in the ride. In my dream there was freedom in my soul as the rider and as the horse. There was no separation; our beings were one.

Shamu

The Blue Moon Rose and Burgundy Rose

Parents
My dad and mom were marvelous. I pray, daily, to them.
I pray from my heart and soul.

Someday I will have to say goodbye,
watching them pull away in their beige Chrysler,
the car jammed with things they can't do without;
clothes for winter, clothes for spring,
golf clubs, T.V., electric fry pan, thermos of decaf,
shovel, blankets and candles, "Just in case."
My father has his briefcase of crossword puzzles,
dictionaries, and computer print-out sheets of answers,
Mother her stash of murder mysteries, the body lifeless
in the opening chapters, spirit vanished.
Miles into the lulling journey, Dad veers
momentarily, not paying attention to the road
or to Mom complaining about the thermostat.
His fingers squeeze the steering wheel.
Someday I will have to wave goodbye,
hoping their route bends into dazzling light.

February 8, 1993

Carole with her parents and Hans

Hidden Place

My hidden place,
the collage in my closet.
Fabric of creamy white background
large peach flowers with olive stripes for leaves;
pale yellow, shades of beige in a sport-weight yarn;
deep yellow angora yarn, twisted cables for a cardigan;
sunspice wool;
black challis with tiny coral, gold and ivory flowers,
gold rope buttons, someday a dress;
white crepe de Chine with a lustrous leaf design,
someday a loosely fitting long-sleeve blouse.
Anxious hands rearrange the skeins of yarn,
each of the soft folds of fabric
an elaborate betrayal of mourning.

February 19, 1992

Horsemen's Horseman—Hans Senn

I love my husband, Hans. Hans had a relationship with horses that was unique and I was the special one to be able to observe this. He had the ability to see what others could not, the horse's spirit. He had the ability to set in action the release of their spirit to allow them to fly. Hans passed from this world on November 10, 2010, at the age of 85. A dear friend from the riding world, Sandra Knaeble, was able to put together words to describe Hans' amazing abilities. I couldn't agree more with the light she shone on Hans' life journey.

A Celebration of Hans' Life by Sandra Knaeble
One of the things Hans often told me was "have a plan." Those of you who were his students—and anyone who really knew him couldn't help being a student of sorts—those of you who were his students will probably remember him saying this.

Have a plan. Winners have a plan, losers have excuses.

Now one might conclude from this that Hans was very rigid in his thinking: that he went around all day with "a plan" and followed it.

And yes, in the external sense, Hans lived in a very deliberate, orderly way. There was, as he would say, no guessing.

If he said a horse was 16.1, then it was 16.1. If he said he would meet you at noon, well you had better be there by 11:59.

But internally, that is, when it came to thinking about horses and riders, the pendulum swung the other direction and orderly structure gave way to a most incredible free play, bounded not by rules but by attention to the moment.

I can explain it best this way. In Zen Buddhism one of the objects of all that sitting around cross-legged on cushions is to train the mind to be quiet. Why? So that in regular life, when you are up walking around, you can react to what is happening AS it is happening, in the moment, and not be thinking about lunch when you are riding a horse.

Hans was a superb practitioner of this art of mindfulness. I know because each lesson with Hans was an experience of thinking as Hans thought. Of meeting the individual moment as it arose.

"Non-stop," as he liked to say. "Non-stop."

It was living in THIS stride. THIS instant of pressure with the outside rein. THIS soft glance into the turn.

Hans was able, with his quiet voice and critical eye, to perfectly translate each individual moment on the horse so that the student was living and riding in the perfect moving present.

The present which arises now, and NOW, and NOW.

Because of his genius, I was able to ride better, far better, than I am actually able to ride. It was a miracle of sorts: to somehow be better than you are. I will miss that.

I will also miss his unconventional take on convention. Hans said he didn't really want a memorial service, which is why we have taken such pains to call this gathering of friends something else—a "celebration," a "time of tribute."

But as I was thinking of this quirk of his, it suddenly flashed upon me that this was a logical extension of his philosophy: it was not that he disliked memorials *per se*, but he didn't want to be bothered with his own because it would occur in the non-existent (for him) future and be about the non-existent (except in memory) past.

But we are here. Now. In this stride, in this beautiful present—non-stop—remembering a man whom we all miss. So there, Hans. Despite your prediction, you ARE here. IN every one of us.

One more thing. Hans often said to me "people aren't grateful enough." Gratitude. An emotion of the present. An emotion that rises up to meet us as we realize the impossible perfection of the here and now.

I am grateful, so very grateful, to have known you, Hans.

Thanks for being here.

Hans

Instantly I liked
your approach, unbridled thoughts
rush onto the page.

When riding horses
I want them unrestricted
as unbridled thoughts.

Trusting to instinct,
horses ridden unrestrained,
unbridled thoughts rush.

February 11, 1992

Love Song

After my brain aneurysm, I feel I am sitting like one of Hans' horses, having my spirit be seen and allowed to fly. I am surrounded by earth angels that continue to support me and my spirit.

Anne Gerber is my Speech-Language Pathologist who has helped me to find my voice. Resurrecting my thoughts into words. Moving me from speaking only in vowels to having complete words, phrases, and sentences. Connecting me with my friends and loved ones through email communication. A friend that accompanies me, through patience and encouragement, to finding my soul.

Carol Warren. I love Carol. She has provided me with stability and is one of my primary caretakers. I am grateful. She has provided the foundation necessary to explore who I am. Her sainthood rescued me from my life at a nursing home. When she first took me in, I was fed from a feeding tube. I did not speak and was heavily medicated. She pushed me to move beyond these barriers through her faith in me. She returned me to being whole.

Jody Hop. She also has opened her home to me and is one of my primary caretakers. She nourishes me through her gift and passion with whole and nutritious food. Encouraging me to improve my walking and standing. Takes me out on trips to the store, out to eat, and to performances giving my spirit flight in the real world. We have a special friendship, a sisterhood, bound in our losses of our loves, Bobby and Hans. She keeps me going and stimulates my mind through conversations and sharing of books.

Merry Lea Slomkowski is my knitting partner. She has helped keep my hobby alive, allowing me inspiration through sharing with me her knitting projects.

Wayne Wood is a dear friend who visits me twice a month. He files my fingernails. He fills my birdfeeders. Wayne is a wonderful handyman who fixes my lift when it breaks and my shower chair. We watch movies together and go out to eat. Wayne passed away on July 6, while I was writing this little book. I miss his companionship dearly.

Cindy Hansen I met while riding at Hans'. We rode the same thoroughbred, Warum. Our friendship began through this bond. She has been by my side through everything. She has taken over my finances after I lost Hans.

Nan Cowin is Cindy's partner, whom I also met through Hans. We rode Kerry, a warmblood, together. She is a dear friend that also cares for my finances since Hans has passed.

Emilio DeGrazia is my mentor and friend. We met when I was a student and he my professor at Winona when I was twenty. He challenged my intellect and continues to do so, through his editing help with my memoir.

Buz is a high school friend that I recently reconnected with while writing my memoir. He has been a sounding board through my writing process. Reading my chapters and asking me thought-provoking questions to have me dig deeper. I am thankful that our paths have crossed again.

Orval Harris Bucker represents heaven to me. My vision, while in a coma, is of Orval as a real lover gifted to me. As my guardian angel, my lover. I left the vision holding space for this meeting of two souls. Knowing I had to pay vigil to it comforting me hourly, daily. Yearning for this depth of love, nurturing-passion to return. My brain, my faith committed, creating hope to live. I question if this type of passion, this space, is to be met now or beyond.

Ann Bleeker is part of my recent companion care team and the mother of Emily Bleeker. Ann has a kind heart. I look forward to our time together because she makes me laugh. Emily Bleeker is part of my companion care team. Her no-nonsense attitude I respect. It keeps me within my bounds.

Linda Schmitt is part of my companion care team. She takes extra good care of my nails since my dear friend Wayne passed away. Linda shares stories about the teenagers she trains in driver's education. It makes me want to drive with Linda. Linda is the mother of Julia, who also visits me.

Karen Olszewskie is part of my companion care team and is the wife of a preacher. I love her gentle spirit and stories about her sweet children.

Julia Engelman is a nurse and also in the National Guard. I love her take-charge personality. Her husband also serves in the military.

Madeline Brugler. I love my weekly visits with Madeline. Her youthfulness and free spirit make me feel free.

Nell Alt is a dear friend who was one of Hans' riding students. Over the years, she has read and knit with me. She is the keeper of my books and brings me new ones from time to time. She has three beautiful children and a fourth on the way.

Dillion is the mother of Nell and also a good friend. Sending me pictures of her family and emails. I look forward to her visits.

Ideally, I will die when I am 94, in the spring. It will be a beautiful death. ("Ideally, I will be 94. Spring. Will beautiful.")

Amen.

I had a repetitive dream with Shamu, Orval, Hans, and me. Shamu and I were trotting and cantering in a dressage show at the fairgrounds. Hans was coaching me and Orval was sitting in the bleachers holding my horse blanket. I was in heaven.

Amen.

September 27, 2012

Orval Harris Bucker with a foal

A Woman's Voice Keeps Haunting Me
Carole's Journal 1994–1995

The writing in this section includes journal entries written by Carole from November 6, 1994 to January 12, 1995. During this time, Carole was living at Helvetia Stables with Hans Senn, whom she married on December 4, 1993. This was a time of healing—both physical and emotional—and of profound introspection. During this time, too, she began caring for Shamu, a horse who had been abused by a previous owner. Carole suffered her brain aneurysm and went into a coma on March 19, 1995.

From a letter to Emilio DeGrazia, December 4, 1994

Hans and I are selling our farm! The purchase agreement has been signed and the closing date is set for December 22nd. Although this is definitely what we both wanted to happen, the selling process itself caused me to feel uprooted, and at times, panic stricken.

This farm has been such a sanctuary for me, my little piece of Switzerland, orderly (not a blade of grass or plank from a wooden fence out of place), clean, peaceful, and adorned with nothing but the finest, most athletic horses imaginable, all for me to ride and play with, nurture. I'm just realizing as I write this how aristocratic and self-assured this sounds. You may not want to know me, after all ... but that essentially is the difficulty; the cost of maintaining this place as fiercely independent as Hans is and with his Olympic standards of quality.

Literature is starting to have more of a pull on me now, so that's another reason for wanting to make this big change. Hans has hundreds of wonderful stories about horses and the horse business that I want to record. It really seems important.

If perhaps you could help me with a few of your thoughts. I might even say that literature has finally become my biggest, all-consuming passion, rather than the horses. I've switched priorities, and it's so scary! (Don't worry, I'm not thinking in terms of publishing or making money—it is the aesthetics which are important.)

—*Carole Jayne*

Carole with a goat

Carole's Journal

November 6, 1994

A woman's voice keeps haunting me the last few days. I know I've heard the voice before, but I can't quite get close enough to make a connection or association. Then, too, I've been hearing Vivaldi's "Four Seasons" over and over again in my head. Plus headaches, dizziness, nausea, you name it. I keep asking myself what my deeper self is trying to tell me, what is my conscious mind not open to? How am I stopping this information from coming forth? *Is the deeper part of myself becoming more forceful?* That would be a welcome influence.

Could it be Laura's sister, Judith? A woman I've never met?

Horse Spirit

The hogs were so thin that they trotted like coyotes. This was my father speaking about the Dust Bowl years…

More from my father about how one farmer he knew [who] lived in the hay loft of his barn, and through the cracks in his floor he could see the hog stabled below. He (my father) was on a threshing crew once, and while most of the crew had to stay in the barn at night, Dad was invited to stay in the farmer's house. However, the bedbugs were so bad that Dad stayed in the farm house only one night, electing to sleep with the others in the barn.

November 28, 1994

The snowmobiles, after the first snowfall of the season, sound like the howl of coyotes. They move in packs, at night, also.

November 29, 1994

The Death of Flowers

Is there a connection between my "loose leg," which Hans is disturbed by and criticizes me often for in my riding lessons, and the "looseness" I feel between my conscious self and my subconscious? I don't feel "whole"; my important issues within my subconscious mind can't seem to find pathways to the surface. Yet I know that part of my mind is working so hard. Last night Hans said I was talking in my sleep most of the night, and I could feel a headache developing during the middle of the night also.

* *I need more connectedness and intensity of experience, stronger connection with my legs when riding.*

Is riding well a pathway to the un- (or sub) conscious? Step by step moving forward?

December 14, 1994

I have resolved to take care of my passions, like children, and not abort them. "What a beautiful choice." The violent thoughts as well as the desired, beautiful ones.

That anger I feel, what anger I'm giving life to! What will it, in turn, create? A hostile, troubled character? A poem which tears open a thought, a poem which rips open a chest and pulls out a heart? (Remember that dream of a surgeon sawing open a breast bone and lifting out a heart?)

Perhaps I have a need for much *rougher* prose or poetry than I had been anticipating. I've been wanting to write something jewel-like, but maybe what I *want* isn't exactly the point.

The hatchet sank into my knee. My hands were numb from the vibrations of peeling the bark from oak fence posts all day long. First I crouched from the pain, then when I stood up I was so dizzy. It was a beautiful evening in summer. A weightless sky. A light yellow, indistinct sun, a washed-out blue and my lover didn't want to stop what he was doing up on the hill in order to help. So I walked down the ridge road myself and found the simple stream, not much of a stream really. I sat in it in my blue jeans. I tore the leg off of one where I had sliced into my knee, and watched the blood make a delicate weave with the water. The water and sky the same empty color, like 7-Up.

"Everything that's there, belongs."

Peeling Bark from Oak Fence Posts

The sun was indistinct, an erased Christmas tree ornament of the palest fragile glass with spokes radiating from an oblong center of densest gold. The water and sky were empty of color except for the delicate weave of blood which turned pink and disappeared. The hatchet had slipped from my numb wrists and hands and sunk into my knee. The dull hatchet blade sank into my knee.

(You've described what happened, now you must leave that and go somewhere else. This is where you need an angel.)

The blood in the water like white paper stained with ink, like little claws moving through the fibers.

A fence to hold in the mule, which worked only partially. When he was content, he'd stick around, when he felt like traveling he would jump right out.

* *A poem that tears open in the middle* ... tears into the chaos.

"Your idea of slow and my idea of slow are not the same."

* Think about some of those freaky fears I have.

The Christmas ornament was a star, a fragile piece of molded glass, with an oblong center and etc. But I was thinking of our sun, during daylight.

December 15, 1994

The tall, extremely tall, pine with softly drooping branches covered with snow.

She was burdened (or blessed) with a pearl choker around her neck. The strands of pearls in front were numerous, and much in the shape of something an African, man or woman? might wear. The Plumed Warrior.

Choky, * choking, chokingly. *

December 16, 1994

Sheepy Shop. The owner of the store and her ruined project.

* The "Sox Appeal." Knitting Class.

* God's Palm. Electric blankets. Children. Wallpaper—how to do it, or hire it done. Turkeys/How their husbands sleep.

The finery of a crocheted glove, on a feminine hand, the shadow of branches on the deep lavender snow, a quiet walk at night, God's palm. Patiently waiting. Tea. The snow is the crocheted threads, double crochets, the shadow of treeless branches, from the trunk forming outwards, are the fine lines on a palm, from the base of the thumb;

(She must be stroking a cat)

(She must be waiting for tea)

* Do not let Hans render me helpless.

* In Winona, write to Emilio, Peggy Tweedy.

(Shadow boxing) fanning outward to the first big arc in the middle of the palm. The row of trees, all God's hands, lining the driveway (softly stroking a cat)

The Fabric Patch

The story about the woman in the fabric store who has waited on me several times, and one time on Homecoming Day she mentioned how conservative her boss was, and how that afternoon her daughter had come into the store dressed as a punk rocker, and the daughter bumped right into her boss. What did he think?

* One thing I love about women is that they can strike up a warm, loving conversation with a perfect stranger in the most unlikely of circumstances. In a public restroom, in a horse stable, in a store, example, asking an opinion on a style or color. In a yarn shop, carrying on a big conversation about a color or a texture…one woman remembered how I had picked out a soft yellow yarn 5 years earlier. They noticed how the flecks of color in the socks I was knitting were knitting up into a confetti pattern. I look up and smile.

How the owner hit two deer on the way home. The deer meat was given to a homeless shelter. These women are rich with details.

My angel has been helping me! You've answered my call!

* Remember that bad experience with John Judson, how when I was in his office, I must have acted nervous or was actually crying about something (what?) and he said, "Don't do this to me." Like his needs were so much more important than mine. A creative writing teacher said this!

* No trust at all. Blind trust.

* Wings of desire.

The Stoa family and their violent streak.

Thank you, Angel.

* The sun was a hydrangea blossom pale hammered like silk

the sky a sheet of tin

the texture of a hammered silk house

Continue in those rhythms.

* The sun is a hydrangea blossom,

The sky a scrap of hammered silk.

December 17, 1994

The Lessons of King Lear: Folly—Wisdom

Shamu did really well today. Riding him as a hunter. Perhaps it is not good for him to be constantly "dressaged."

Hans and I had several "discussions" today, and we each caused pain, I believe. Toward the end, Hans reminded me that he "nursed me" for several years, comforting me through years of screaming in my sleep. Somehow I was able to tell him that I still haven't regained trust, no matter how much I may want to. The deeper levels of my heart don't trust. I told him that if he had a better understanding of psychology that he might understand what I mean.

That lack of trust, having that, has been my secret. I never thought that I would tell that to Hans. I was hoping to spare him. I have no idea what he thinks.

I felt shot full of holes.

Line of poetry:

"I've been shot full of holes."

* Remember how I pushed Jay on several occasions?

I also told Hans how he's not an easy man. "You just aren't." He then said that I was not an easy woman.

(to be expanded on later. a.m. wearable art)

The snow is like a beaded mohair sweater.

Beaded pearl.

First the brown and white scarf in garden stitch. Mom keeps in the car for emergencies.

* The horse blanket I tried to knit as a little girl. White with apple-green hearts. Now in a tapestry, without the hunting scenes.

Valor, etc. * Women have valor. *

December 21, 1994

I have run out of time this evening but I thought I'd quickly get down a few notes. I took my last box of Iowa things to the Goodwill store today: a nice turntable and speakers, a cassette player and an old radio. I believe all of it is in good working order.

I feel that I have become transformed within the past week: I don't feel well when I don't write at least half an hour every day. That expression has suddenly become such an important part of my life. I am trying to do right by those inner workings and find a connection.

Remember some of those pizza suppers I had with Jay were in downtown Decorah? Was it at Godfather's Pizza? I wonder what we kept talking about. (I was going to write a book called "The Language of Horses.")

He must have suffered with a lot of pain.

Remember how, that time my parents came down to stay overnight in Decorah, I went back to the farm to stay with Jay: How incredibly dangerous that was. Was that the same night that he insisted we go to the Harlan's for a lengthy talk?

December 23, 1994

I didn't ride today. I needed a day of rest, up to a point. I still lunged????? a few horses, did two loads of laundry, moved the last of my things from the east apartment and did some reading—that's what I consider a sick day. We went through with the sale [of the farm] and it's one of the most painful things I've ever done. The feelings of grief will last a long time, I think. How can we have sold the farm?

But at the same time, I believe that this is the true beginning of our marriage. We've spoken about so many things this past week. I told Hans that I first fell in love with him in 9th grade, when I came up to buy a horse. A week ago, he reminded me how he nursed me "Back to Health," getting me through all those nightmares. We've had frank discussions about finances, and what it is going to be like for the next several years.

That image I had when I was ill this morning: Peoples' mouths, tense with anger, extreme anger——mouthy turns into a festering sore—— lips, sexuality.

This is one of the first times that I've allowed an ugly image to happen. I've so much believed in the beautiful.

It seems, again, that I must write, now, every day. I become physically ill when I've skipped writing in the evening before. My deep thoughts and voices are insisting on their freedom. Kari, the horse, has "thoughts" also, and he supposedly is my "twin." How does this correlate with my situation? The static, the inability to express the tenseness, the oversensitivity to noise and distractions, and how all these things make him seemingly less trainable than other horses.

Remember Jan's thought about how she thinks jumping is more of a 50-50 proposition as opposed to dressage. Depending on the horse's judgment.

Challenge: How to allow for the horse's expressiveness.

December 24, 1994

From Jamestown this morning I heard the tortured cry "It's too late for me—save yourselves."

Christmas Day, 1994

The concept of "Inversions"

* an inverted horse

* Shakespeare's *King Lear*

* how in my poetry the choice of words could somehow exhibit the inversion

The fascination I have with car emblems. As I'm driving I focus in on them as cars drive by me in the other lanes. I feel a "kinship" with other Volkswagen drivers and owners. Remember the young man who stopped me on the streets in Stillwater and we discussed Volkswagens? He was really an expert, and he loved my new car.

Working Titles for My Own Story
* Horse Killer
* The Assassinated Horse
* An Assassination of Horses
* The Murdered Horses

Get a list of their names. Look at the folder on the bottom of Jay's briefcase.

The horses and myself were shot in the same way. However, the horses were not as fortunate as I. They lost their lives.

* A non-linear memoir, bits of the past, imagery welling up and affecting the present life of the troubled woman.

The Dangerous Saltwell colt named "Praise the Lord" and how that owner cruelly relayed information about the murdered horses.

The woman didn't realize that Jay had murdered the horses until she herself had been shot. The sheriff's revelations (They knew) (So much of the town knew, although she insisted to me that "He wouldn't touch a fly.") Also, remember in one of Marjorie's drunken episodes she told Jay that she became an alcoholic because "Jay was nuts." That's why. She didn't know how to cope with it. At the time, I thought she was merely being cruel, trying to hurt him. But there was truth in it. He was nuts. But I cared for him deeply.

Vague stories about the "mob" wanting to come after Jay and that's why the horses were killed.

* This group of horses seemed to live on in Jay's mind long after the death of them. He had them shipped to various places in Kentucky, Florida, Arkansas or California, and he still owned them. He had imaginary talks on the phone with trainers and often their children. Sometimes he would actually talk with a trainer on the phone, but it was probably about life and race track life in general. Or he would take imaginary flights on charter airplanes to visit his animals, dine with the trainer, etc.

Jay

Stroking the cats, his loving behavior with the cats and his care of them.

His mad language. His soft belly, exposed because the buttons on the lower part of his shirt were always unbuttoned.

How he tried to sabotage the trip to Minneapolis. With whiskey. He drove the truck through the mud, and mysteriously the left spring on that one side of the trailer was broken. We discovered it halfway up to Minneapolis.

The fire and the tractor. The fire department had to be called out to put out a big grass fire and he was so upset when I asked him to be more careful.

How at one point he asked me to kill him with a knife in my studio apartment.

Remember how jealous Hans became once when he realized that Jay had stayed overnight? And how Hans wouldn't listen to my explanation until later.

* Opening lines: description of the shadows on the snow at night, and then perhaps a description of Marjorie sitting on her throne, the fuchsia chair covered with a powder blue satin blanket. The rotting dead mice underneath. How she must have looked when she was younger. Crocheted gloves and big hats.

The first time I met her she was lying on the cement, drunk, and I believe she had broken a hip (one of the first times).

How she took a piss outside a major liquor store in La Crosse. She had only a light, see-through "chiffon" nightgown, cut to knee length (roughly), with a scissors.

* The stories of Bob, and the kind of man he was: how he said he and his friends burned a house down after several years of living in it.

A Lear. His dangerousness.

December 26 and 27, 1994

The tips of the birch tree branches looked like they had been dipped in red wine (wine fingernail polish) on a record warm winter day.

Describe the clouds and sky from yesterday.

The flow of energy has to be correct from leg to hand in order to maintain the horse's energy, bend, etc. (I haven't said this right, but I just wanted to get enough down so I wouldn't forget it. Resume on Tuesday morning).

The flow of energy between conscious and "hidden thoughts."

The correlation between A) and B). The horse is like the powerful unconscious.

December 27, 1994

I have had some thoughts today about some of my terror and I wonder how right I am about this. When a terrifying image pops into my mind (example: getting a foot caught in a stirrup and getting dragged, my head being banged around), I just realized that the image is not an expression that has to do with the fear of horses, but perhaps it is that the horse is a symbol that my unconscious or inner thoughts are using to convey a message. Instead of discounting and repressing the image, I believe I should give it more of a viewing, see where it goes, what actions it takes. Would it be the underlying fear of death?

The terrifying part of the image has to do with, not the horse, but the sensation of losing my balance and swinging backward and down. I'd like to push it further and see what fiction can be made of it. A first true voyage. Begin tomorrow.

A fabric store is my museum. The hundreds of bolts of cloth, from rayon challis to crepe de Chine to all the cottons used for piecing quilts.

December 28, 1994

Working titles for a collection of poems:
Listening in the Silence & Deepest Thoughts

I have had some important thoughts about my mother today, especially relating to her insomnia. For as long as I can remember she has been complaining about sleeplessness and she almost always calls herself a "wreck" the next day. This is so much like the ship metaphor I was thinking about a week or so ago. She, at night, seems to be a ship tossed about by the restless, angry seas. The seas are her deepest thoughts, and in this light (in this metaphor) her deepest thoughts are working against her. That's what I have felt all along, and what I've seen: the conflict within my mother between the surface and the deepest thoughts. It is a conflict that she has never resolved. Next time I have a discussion with her I will ask her, "What thoughts are troubling you?" It will be fascinating to hear her response. At times the answer is obvious: One of the children is troubling her. But on many, many occasions there seems to be nothing "out there."

I've had some experience with insomnia also. Especially this fall, I would wake up in a startled state, panicky, heart pounding, unable to breathe. But the difference between my mother and me is that I'm willing to try something different, whatever it takes to solve the problem. Like giving up alcohol. Like examining my thoughts. Like an earnest plea to God or to my angel before slipping away in unconsciousness. The last sentence sounds so silly when it is written down on paper, but I'll try anything, even if the language or technique isn't just right.

My mother adds to the problem also by noise pollution and static. When she falls asleep she insists on listening to the television set, as if wanting something to lull her asleep. Shows like Johnny Carson were a favorite.

The only positive thing is that in late years she has tried to do something constructive with her time when she absolutely could not even lie in bed quietly. She'll read for a while or else work in the kitchen for a while.

I'm pleased with the thoughts I've had today. They may be simplistic, but I do think that I'm starting to get at some of the symbols I've been using all my life.

* When I awoke this morning, my deepest thoughts had been troubling me also. These troubling thoughts have the effect of making me generally afraid of things, life. Remember how frightened I was to ride Bolero around Hans when he was lunging? Instead of concentrating on just riding, I thought some catastrophe was going to happen. Then when Man came in the ring with Orangie I thought Bolero would spook by the gate. But none of these things happened! It was my cynical thoughts!! How much better I could have ridden him if those thoughts wouldn't be there!! That is the challenge before me.

January 2, 1995

A poem in the making!

The walk I take through the barn at night somehow reminds me of the walks I would take through the corridors of the nursing home working the graveyard shifts. The walks I take through the barn every evening are compulsive, as if I have some unfinished business. I listen for the breathing of the horses [as] they are quietly munching their hay. In the nursing home I would tip-toe into the rooms to listen for the breaths of the old people (the residents). If one would hear me, that person would almost always ask for assistance to get to the bathroom or the commode. One night I must not have checked close enough for Bergetta's breathing. She was dead when the morning shift came and began getting everyone ready for breakfast. The home was angry with me, for not finding her sooner. So every evening I check the breathing of the horses, see their shadows in the dark box stalls.

* Danny, the young man who was shot in the neck, I loved him.

* I haven't explored it fully (I don't know how), but having an orgasm makes me cry. At that moment, I'm so alive to the pain within me, as well as the joy.

January 3, 1995

Leaving home—the concept of—Does the analogy of a ship leaving port work? Returning to port?

* Begin discussion about the shooting—material for writing my own story.

In the Decorah Hospital, remember how the nurse said, "He's a goner." And also, they had forgotten to pull the curtain between us, so I could look over at him.

* Before I was lifted into the ambulance, remember how worried I was about losing my—where did this come from—purse? Remember years earlier when my mother bought me a purse and told me to keep my treasures in there. (The small taupe evening bag).

* Perhaps one of the most shattering moments for me was in the Decorah Hospital when Dr. Bakken would not hold my hand, as I was begging him to do. It was bad enough to have to beg, but then to beg and not have him come through for me. I felt like such an outcast at that moment, like I'd have to do this all on my own. The scarlet letter.

Was he a coward? Or was there more to it than that? I believe it was at that moment that I lost all trust, all faith in other humans. (Tell this to Emilio in next letter, the issue of trust).

* Hands are so beautiful. Expressive, useful. One reason I want to write is because it employs my hands. Writing letters to me is a form of hand holding. To carry some of these thoughts further, have I been too heavy-handed at times with the horses because of not letting my hands speak (write) in these other ways?

Remember the *Age of Innocence* (the movie) and how beautifully the passions were expressed through the hands. I saw this movie with Jan!

January 4, 1995

I have been exhausted by my emotions today. Sorrow for the shooting itself and also a sense of longing for a certain kind of love. For the first time, in a way, I've let love touch me, really touch me, and it's a bit overwhelming. What can I do with it? What should I?

I have a history of being loved and not loved at the same time, by the same man. Or I've asked men to love me who aren't capable of it. To me it's a form of dissembling. *Making a pretense of loving the unlovable.* That's all I felt I could do, all the farther I felt I could go. *I've had myself convinced of my limitations, which may not really exist.* For as long as I can remember I've felt that love is something indirect, dissembling. But yesterday I felt the possibility of the directness of love. It's too new. I don't know what to make of it.

He seems to message the bruised part of my brain.

I'd like to write a poem about the office, the comfort of the office.

One of the reasons I wanted to hold Dr. Bakken's hand years ago (in 1986) was that if I did die, I wanted some control over my last vision. I wanted to gaze at an object of beauty. The human hand seemed all that was available, and all its expressiveness. He refused. He refused to comfort me. He refused to let me look at his hand.

I think it was Jay who latched onto me.

January 5, 1995

The piano. She dives into the (?), but resurfaces.

Use this imagery within the poem. Finding the beaded pearl at the bottom of the knitting bag. The array of dark yarns—describe.

What did (does) this experience mean to you?

A big thing in the hospital and afterward was that people kept telling me what experiences meant to *them*. They would relate stories about their family member who had committed suicide, etc. The sheriff and policemen were no different.

January 7, 1995

I don't have much time this something morning (what was that voice I heard, the one that said I wouldn't die yet, not for a long time) not for a long time, but I've wanted to record my thoughts from last night. I've become unstuck from the thoughts about Dr. Bakken. Last night I realized that it wasn't Dr. Bakken that I wanted to connect with, but that it was the Hand of the Creator. But, and this is what has moved me so terribly, the Creator didn't want me at that time. He or It (?) didn't reach for me. For this reason, I want to call this chapter, "Dress Rehearsal."

The description of the aloneness, the helplessness, the nakedness at that moment.

January 12, 1995

Opening line: *Love for me had meant making allowances.*

Note to myself: The Red Ball of the Sun (the serpent's tongue of flame inside the barrel of a gun), the sky, a dark steel (the barrel).

Autumn Thoughts

Anonymous—written by a student at The Loft Literary Center in Minneapolis, Minnesota, after Carole revealed to the class her experience of being shot.

On Thanksgiving Eve seven years will have passed.
Remember the worst part seemed
the neighbors and people from town
going through our house in the days following
the attempted murder, the actual suicide.

Months later I discovered so many things missing:
Cash from my husband's billfold, 35mm cameras,
video equipment, dishes, and my mother-in-law's rings.

When I was recuperating, someone whispered to me
that he knows who took the tools from the shed.
The thief was a Jehovah's Witness, and the thief's
wife was an acquaintance of mine. Her friends
wrote me a long, incoherent letter
wanting to cast out demons.

I've thought a sheriff must have taken
the rifle that my husband hid in the big, white barn.
He phoned me at the hospital; he admired it,
asked if I would sell. He reminded me often that
I would've been blown away
had this been the murder weapon.
To be shot with a .22 caliber pistol
was lucky. I'm lucky.

Remember dwelling upon the loss of those possessions.
It kept me from a greater fear, not only of what he committed
but what he intended to commit. The pistol he borrowed,
the highpowered rifle I didn't know he owned. And
I didn't go with him. He tried to get me to the barn
that day to see the kitten he had found, that he loved.

The kitten, the kitten.

The Making of Carole's Memoir
Anne Gerber

Carole's initial hospitalization and the medical progression that took place for four years prior to her placement in foster care are discussed earlier. Highlighted in the following pages is Carole's journey in speech and language therapy that began after she was placed in private foster care living.

By taking readers through the journey of Carole's struggles and progression with speech and language therapy, I hope to provide an understanding of the steps she took toward writing her memoir and poetry. This is the story of the transformation of a woman whose words were expected to die with her when she was shot by her husband and then later suffered a life-threatening aneurysm.

Carole working on her memoir

Carole faced many obstacles in her efforts to communicate after her aneurysm. Having been with Carole throughout her process, I, as a speech language pathologist and person, was transformed as well.

My journey required letting go of a conditioned model of delivering services that made a set of individual skills the focus of therapy. What emerged was a client-centered approach, with Carole the navigator and I the follower. Carole would say she learned from me, but she has been one of my greatest teachers.

Our Paths Merge

In the spring of 1999, as Carole Stoa Senn was being moved from residential care to her new foster care setting in the home of Carol Hop, I was getting ready to graduate from the master's program in communicative disorders at the University of Wisconsin, Madison. My studies and internships gave me experiences as a provider of therapy in a variety of settings, from in-home private practice to working in subacute care at a Twin Cities trauma hospital. These experiences would play a role in my future work with Carole.

My path crossed Carole's in 2006. I had been working for five years as a Speech Language Pathologist in private practice, primarily serving preschool, school-aged children, and an occasional adult client. My clinical career was filled with objective goal writing and with struggles to persuade insurance companies to provide coverage for my clients. At the time, there was a heavy emphasis on establishing therapy goals using a functional communication model. Goal writing was centered around improving communication for a clients' tasks of daily living in their present environments. Examples of this would be increasing a clients' ability to verbally request what they wanted to eat for breakfast or express their choice of an activity throughout their day. I did not realize it at the time, but my work with Carole would challenge my goal writing skills to reach beyond the boundaries of just daily living tasks alone.

When I met Carole, I was already a lifelong friend of the Hops, Carole's newly acquired foster family. I had first met Jody Hop in high school, and our acquaintance later developed into a close friendship. The Hops, knowing I was a practicing SLP, approached me while I was on maternity leave with my first daughter. Carole, who had tried various speech, language and physical therapies for several years, had lost her desire to participate in them. Carole was known to dismiss therapists if she did not agree with what was being done. Around the time I was on maternity leave, Carole mentioned to her husband Hans that she had a desire to start speech therapy again. After Hans visited with Carole's doctor a referral was made and I was contacted.

Assessing Skills and Direction in Therapy

After initially assessing Carole, I walked away understanding the magnitude of how the stroke affected all areas of her communication (comprehension, expression, speech production, writing, and reading). The biggest challenge for Carole was her deficiency in verbal expression, in particular the clarity of her speech. Carole primarily spoke in vowel sounds, using single words with an occasional attempt at stringing two words together or using the carrier phrase "I would like ____." She had lengthy time delays in initiating expressive communication due to word finding issues and motor speech disturbances that affected her ability to coordinate and sequence the muscles of speech that produce fluid communication. Carole's delays made it difficult for communication partners to stay engaged in the conversation if they were relying on Carole's speech alone. Despite Carole's limitations, she also possessed residual skills that were a tremendous asset to her communication. Carole demonstrated the ability to understand simple written and spoken material, and this made her ability to read and be read to an enjoyable outlet. Her ability to understand far exceeded her ability to express herself.

In her speech and language therapy sessions at the nursing home she had learned to write, with her non-dominant hand, words that she was unable to verbalize. Carole had awareness when others did not understand her, and this awareness allowed her to bridge the communication gap for her listener. During conversation Carole used nonverbal communication to engage her communication partner. She connected beyond the spoken word by making eye contact with others and by using laughter to show that she was following what was being said. Carole also demonstrated the ability to self-correct or show awareness of her errors and even to laugh at herself and others when mistakes were made.

Carole had a rich supportive community that included her two in-home care providers, her husband, and a handful of friends and family that came to visit, to take her on weekly trips to the store, or to eat at local restaurants. Her husband Hans would take her to his home, which was only a mile from where she was living. This gave Carole time to spend with her dog, gather her books or go through her yarn for a current knitting project with a friend.

In the initial phases of meeting with Carole, I spent time talking with her individual care providers, family, and friends in order to understand the strengths and limitations that existed for them when communicating with Carole. Hans wanted to support Carole's efforts to communicate. He said that it was hard for him to understand her most times, but that they had their way of getting along by following a predictable routine when they were together. Carole's extended family expressed curiosity about any advances in technology that might assist Carole with communicating more efficiently. Her caregivers wanted to know what Carole needed so that their daily routines could run more smoothly and allow for more flexibility. When Carole was asked at the time if there was anything specific she wanted to work on in her speech and language therapy, she said, "All," with shouts of cheer.

The next step was to take in all of the information I had collected during the assessment phase to begin to piece together goals and a plan that addressed her various communication needs. After this review period, I had come up with a direction for Carole's speech and language therapy that I wanted to present to her: the use of a speech output device to help her express herself and improve the ability of others to understand her. What I did not realize was that Carole had already been introduced to using such a device and wanted nothing to do with a device speaking for her. Carole made it clear that she wanted to work on using her own voice.

My Internal Unraveling

Carole's request to work on her speech production raised a dilemma for me as a speech language pathologist. What would happen if Carole's direction of therapy did not agree with what I, as the "expert," thought could be done? This dilemma started me questioning what I had learned from my schooling. Neuroscience at the time emphasized allowing one to three months for the peak course of neurological recovery after an aneurysm, with recovery continuing at a slower pace for at least an additional six months. Neuroplasticity, the ability for the brain to form new neuropathways necessary to relearning skills disrupted by brain injury, was also dependent on the severity of the aneurysm and damage to surrounding areas. What I knew from reviewing her medical records was that Carole's stroke was severe and that it had been four years since her aneurysm. As I took into consideration her desire to target her speech production, I started to question if this was a realistic goal. Was I really going to work on teaching her skills to regain the ability to produce speech if scientific studies strongly suggested that physiologically she had passed the window of opportunity? As a speech language pathologist, I was trained to help clients compensate for their lost skills by teaching them alternative means to communicate. Through the use of various augmentative and alternative communication (AAC) systems, the communicator was supposed to rely on means other than their limited oral speech to express themselves. The different forms of AAC systems range from an aided system, which relies on clients using their own body or body language (e.g. facial gesture, pointing) to express their message, to using an aided system that relies on external equipment or tools such as a paper and pencil, pictures, communication boards, or a high-tech voice output device.

At first glance it seemed that the proper scientific approach to Carole's case would have the therapist build up her communication skills by using a unique array of AAC systems to support her communication needs across environments. Oral speech would not be an area to focus on because she was beyond the six-month marker. According to the textbooks, the direction of therapy would be a simple one. My challenge would be how to proceed in therapy while trying to reconcile two worlds which at the time seemed very separate: science and Carole's desires. How could I merge the wishes and desires of my client with what I thought I knew was best for her, according to what science was indicating at the time?

As I wondered if I could essentially detach from what I thought was best for Carole's communication development, something happened. Other important factors that needed to be considered when determining the direction of Carole's therapy slowly came to mind. Clearly, both internal and external factors unique to Carole's case weighed on her ability to acquire skills in her previous speech and language sessions. So, what were these factors? Four years after the stroke, Carole's body was still struggling to heal itself physically. She had lived in environments she did not find optimal, and she had been heavily medicated for pain and seizure activity. Her nutrition was measured through protein shakes and pureed food. It was interesting that her desire and willingness to work on her speech and language came back after she moved beyond these major physical and environmental hurdles.

As I pulled together these various points of view, it became clear that I didn't know if she would be able to learn new speech skills four years after her aneurysm until we tried. We proceeded with a "Let's write up some speech goals and see what happens" attitude, bringing with us unanswered questions and Carole's strong desire to use oral speech to communicate. And that's when progress began, two individuals learning to trust. For me, the process required a willingness to walk forward while letting go of my "clinician knows best" attitudes, and the willingness to keenly listen and observe as I opened myself to Carole's guidance.

This was a dance, one that allowed Carole to be in the lead while I measured and collected data to make sure my heart was not just following hope.

Speech and Language Improve—More Questions

Carole and I started by trying to fine tune her speech production skills. Specific skills were important to develop if she was to experience successful speech production. Her aneurysm had permanently damaged key physiological operations. To varying degrees, these physiological blocks affected Carole's ability to voluntarily control the movement of the roof of her mouth and portions of her tongue, and the timing of her vocal chords and respiratory muscles. This meant that there would be certain speech sounds Carole would not be able to produce, and that her speech quality would have a quiet and dampened nasal quality. Despite these known "unchangeables," also available were a host of other speech sounds and skills that, if she could learn, would improve Carole's speech intelligibility and meet Carole's desire to work on her speech.

How Carole learned to produce new speech sounds is a perfect representation of her tenacity and playful spirit. The initial stages of her therapy focused on increasing her awareness that, although she believed she was producing full words, she in fact was leaving off all consonants (example, "dog" sounded like "ahhh"). Her speech was a string of vowel sounds that left the listener working hard to understand what she was trying to say.

Throughout the course of a year, Carole relearned how to produce individual speech sounds by grouping the sounds together and by trying to determine where the sound was produced in her mouth, and what part of the mouth was producing the sound (e.g. Was the tongue or were the lips used in making the "b" sound, and was it made in the front or back of the mouth?). She also focused on the kinesthetic feeling of the sound within her mouth (e.g. Is air sneaking out between the lips as it does when producing "f," or is air bursting out from the lips as when producing a "p"?) Carole would point to picture representations to show that she understood.

The mirror was her best friend during this time, as she watched herself close her lips to produce a "b," or raise her tongue to the roof of her mouth to produce a "t" sound. We attempted to make this time of building the foundational speech skills as playful as we could. Carole used lip gloss to practice feeling the sensation of her lips, and she rubbed them together to spread the gloss around.

Once her awareness of sensation and of the movement of her speech muscles (lips, tongue, palate) was established, we started pairing individual consonants with vowel sounds to produce words. Carole literally felt her way into producing words, a process that to us seems automatic. To make these stages meaningful, Carole often practiced cooing and stringing sounds together while holding my baby daughter Hazel in her arms. Carole's rigid arm posture made the perfect cradle for holding a baby. Carole would light up during these interactions, as would my nine-month-old daughter. She also worked on producing the names of her loved ones with more clarity, moving from only producing the vowel sounds in names like Mom, Tom and Bob to adding the initial and final consonants so that others could understand her better. We read poems together from her favorite poets like Rilke and Emerson and her own work written before the aneurysm, so she could feel and hear herself speaking in longer sentences.

Throughout the first year, Carole made improvements in small but important ways. She was able to produce some basic consonant sounds that she was not able to produce before, and this helped her to say the names of loved ones and talk about items in her room with more clarity. Her husband and caregivers said they were able to understand her 25 percent better, and unfamiliar listeners 20 percent better. What the year showed me was that Carole was ambitious, making gains and still motivated. She seemed empowered and brighter. Each time we met she greeted me with enthusiasm and determination.

What remained, however, was the limitation that her stroke left on her motor abilities to produce longer and complex multi-syllable words and certain key consonant sounds. From a neurological perspective, she could not get around these challenges. But by using other means, such as writing words down and pointing to words in a communication book, she would be able to compensate. Aware of her limits with speech production, the challenge I faced was how to further improve her ability to be understood by both familiar and unfamiliar communication partners. Could Carole expand her language to different types of words to make her communication richer and her engagement in various communication situations more intimate? And further, would development of her language abilities translate into greater verbal and/or written output?

From these questions and challenges new goals arose. For the first year, Carole primarily spoke in single words. She spent the second year using communication boards to expand her understanding of language, expressive vocabulary, and production of different phrase and sentence types. Carole's ability to use language with more flexibility was targeted as she was challenged to put words together to make a richer array of communication messages from asking questions, commenting, requesting information, initiating conversation and closing a conversation. When Carole was provided with visual aids, words or phrases written on a page, they helped her retain new phrase structures. Using this system, she was able to point to or speak the phrases she wanted to say. She used words from her immediate environment to set the stage for her therapy, and practiced phrase and sentence structures that would assist in conveying messages basic to her daily living tasks (For example, "Please, move it next to the bookshelf"). She had communication templates to use for various communication partners that were specific to that person. This allowed her access to conversational sentences that were specific to whomever she was speaking. She would ask her husband how his knees were, and her friend Dillon if there were any new stories from the art museum.

Carole's prior knowledge of literature and poetry could be seen when we worked on identifying words by grammatical types (pronouns, adjectives, verbs). Carole lit up when she was pushed to expand what she was saying by adding words of feeling or description, or pizzazz and texture as we would call them. What I began to see over time was that Carole did start to incorporate these new phrases and sentence structures into her spontaneous communication both verbally and in written form. Although the amount and ease of her verbalizations were limited, she expanded on the types of verbalizations, paying compliments, commenting on conversations, and adding to conversation with relevant responses.

The consistency of her verbal responses, however, was unpredictable, and this required her communication partner to still play an active role in assisting Carole. With the expansion of her language, questions arose again. Carole seemed content with the ways she communicated with others. She gravitated toward using both her speech and facial gestures, writing words on paper that she could not verbally access, and on occasion using her communication boards. Because she had achieved some satisfaction as a communicator, I questioned if we had hit a wall in her need for continued speech and language services. But with the advancement of technology came questions about how Carole's communication could be improved by connecting her via email to a virtual community of friends and family. After talking with Carole, she expressed her interest in getting a laptop to reach out to family and friends.

Expanding Connection in a Virtual Community

At this point in Carole's therapy we developed a new focus—expanding Carole's written expression and language goals through use of a laptop, and connecting her with family through the internet and email. This new focus pushed Carole to expand her memory for a sequence of nonverbal tasks, such as starting up the computer, and logging online. She also was challenged to pick out the main points within email messages she received, and was taught how to respond to emails in engaging ways. Carole began to layer various communication techniques that she had been working on over the years to get to her goal of creating a written email message. We developed new simple communication boards that provided visual steps and choices about what sentences would work best for the message she was creating. She worked on layout—the construction of an email from the heading, introductory sentence, main body and conclusion. She moved from needing direct help with formulating messages to independently constructing simple email responses verbally or written in her notebook, with me acting as her typing hands. She worked on developing cognitive flexibility by having to decide the best response to give for the various conversations that would arise from her growing virtual community. Carole made connections with old horse riding friends, lost high school and college classmates, and relatives that lived afar.

There were limitations with the laptop, however. Given Carole's motor impairments that affected the speed of movement of her hands, independent typing was a challenge. Although she could type, the time and energy it took did not make it practical. Typing her name into the computer alone could take up to five minutes, and if she made a mistake…forget it. She still required the direct help of an outside facilitator to get her messages successfully across in the virtual world. But one positive outcome of her working on formulating connected bodies of text was that her handwriting skills became more independent and complex. She started to write "to do" lists while alone and had them waiting to go over with me when we met for speech therapy. She also was able to independently lay out a simple email message in writing and have it completed by our next session together.

Despite her physical limitations, writing email messages and connecting with friends and family were very rewarding for Carole. She often would cheer and say, "Did it!" as she hit "Send" on the computer. Carole began to see herself connecting with others and expressing her ideas and thoughts. Old stories would surface that she would share with me or want to share with those she was emailing. And I believe this started to stir something even deeper inside Carole.

Desire to Write a Memoir

It was around this time in 2010 that Carole first brought up the desire to write a memoir. I do admit: I had serious concerns about how we were going to get this to happen. Despite improvements in her communication, we were not yet writing connected sentences, let alone paragraphs or a full body of work. I started questioning how and if she could do this. And then I realized the beauty that this request could provide. Aside from being able to create rich goals for expanding her communication skills, she would also be able to work within a parameter that was hers.

From the start, Carole knew the names of chapters, and the titles of the poems she had written prior to her aneurysm. It was as if she had been sitting on the idea of writing a memoir for some time. She began outlining chapters by writing single words or phrases on a page. In the beginning, they were often randomly placed on the page with circles and arrows connecting her thoughts. I acted as her typing hands and facilitator. I prompted her for more information by asking series of questions intended to make connections with what she had written, or to help her expand on what she was saying if her written message was not clear. If the words were not flowing on a particular day, I would provide Carole with verbal choices of the directions I thought she was trying to take with the written piece. She would touch my hand to indicate if it was choice one or choice two.

Carole's determination and engagement in the process of refining what she wrote were astonishing. To further assist Carole in expressing the editing changes, we developed together a communication board that contained specific editing words or phrases, such as "change this," "move this," "this doesn't sound right," "add a comma," "lower case," "erase," "new paragraph." Carole would scan the page and point to the editing changes she wanted to make. Once she selected her edit request, I would retype the sentence and read it aloud as Carole would follow along visually scanning the written text. At this point she would either accept the sentence, request more changes, or reject it altogether to start the process over.

Those who know Carole's determination and perfectionism would understand how great it felt when Carole would finally signal that we had found the correct words to convey her thoughts. When the words were not right, Mrs. Carole Jayne definitely let me know, and would not let it rest!

By the end of our writing meetings Carole was producing outlines as "homework" to do between our sessions together. These outlines often contained complete sentences. She also began to verbalize words and phrases that needed editing, not relying solely on having to point to the editing changes prewritten in her communication board. Carole's ability to self-correct increased as she read words, phrases, and sentences in an outline she wanted me to write down. This was amazing to see as Carole's self-correction of omitted words or use of incorrect words to this point took frequent prompting by me: "Carole does this sound correct?" The little connecting words and articles, such as "and," "the," and "a" that Carole consistently left out of both her verbal and written language also started to emerge through the process of writing her memoir. Her eagerness was remarkable. Throughout sometimes long therapy sessions, Carole remained focused. She would request me to contact Emilio, her writer friend, for editing help, and would come up with outlines of what her emails should say. At last the therapy techniques and skills Carole had been working with were coming together to enable her to create her memoir. The inner part of Carole that had been locked inside was not only alive, but was beginning to come out.

It was during the memoir writing process that there was a direct shift in who was leading the flow of our time together. What I notice, in reflecting back, is that this was the time I released my attachment to guiding the therapy and opened myself to Carole's process and direction. She was becoming her own guide in her journey toward her own memoir, and I was becoming the assistant, using my tools and skills as speech language pathologist to help her achieve her goal.

Improving Independence with an iPad and Poetry

As Carole plugged along writing chapters in her memoir, I was also looking for ways to further improve her independence through the use of her laptop and emails. She was beginning to type, but the process was so fatiguing it disrupted her ability to convey her messages. With the hope to finding a way for Carole to become more independent, I attended a Closing the Gap conference in Minneapolis in 2011. Technology resources promised increased independence for children and adults with disabilities by assisting them to freely navigate the virtual world. I wanted to see how advancements in technology influenced assistive devices, and if there was a better match for Carole than the laptop, keyboard and mouse she was currently using. After the conference, Carole began using an iPad, which helped her improve navigation speed and independence with email programs and the internet. I also learned of various educational apps that could be used in therapy that could assist Carole's memory, word finding, and sentence structure development.

At this conference, I also attended a workshop on poetry writing called "Poetry Power: From Emergent to Conventional Writing." I had no idea how helpful this workshop would be to enable Carole to reclaim her sense of identity. The workshop provided me with some poetry writing activities and books to further support Carole's poetry writing process.

Carole was excited about this new way to spend our time together. We were used to reading her old poetry, an activity that kept her thinking about the poetry she had written years earlier. But by reading about new poetry styles and going through various poetry writing exercises she began to redefine her poetry style to fit her present self. The rebirth of Carole's poetry writing started out with heavy guidance and cuing that directed Carole toward poetry structure and word selection. She started by writing down single topic words that interested her—horses, chandeliers, birds. She would begin by choosing one word that she wanted to expand on. Another technique was to ask Carole to use her hearing to tap into her surrounding environment. I would invite her to close her eyes, thereby eliminating external visual distractions, and ask her to take a minute to reflect on what she heard around her. Carole would often come up with three or four things she heard (children, wind, Vivaldi). She then would be asked to read over the words she came up with and choose which word she wanted to expand on. She also was walked through various prompted questions to encourage the expansion of her phrases (e.g. "Where were the children as the wind blew?" or "How did the wind feel as it blew?"). I would write down her response and Carole would read along, making edits.

The progressive development of Carole's poetry is evident. She moved from needing the step-by-step word assistance to writing poetry independently, often with me not even being present. Her current process involves using a dictionary to help her find words if she is having difficulty, or looking up phrases that she wants to expand.

Producing one poem can take Carole one or two days (on average four to six hours total). One would think this would be frustrating, but Carole shrugs her shoulders when we talk about the time and she says "So?" She cheers and smiles, larger than life, when we read her new poetry creations and usually says, "Read it again," as she laughs. Then she says, "I love it."

Carole's ability to learn and retain new skills has allowed her to increase her typing speed through using the touch screen technology and automatic word and phrase guess systems on her iPad. Although handwriting continues to be Carole's most efficient means of conveying her email messages or poetry writing if someone is not there to type for her, the iPad has allowed her easy access to getting online.

She now can independently check her email, access Facebook, clean up her inbox, file messages she wants to keep, and compose simple email messages.

What Carole Taught Me

When I worked in a clinical setting I faced the challenge of trying to keep a balance between providing meaningful functional services for the children and adults I worked with while keeping up with the demands of caseload numbers, writing assessments and therapy goals. I also had to confront insurance companies insistent on denying coverage for clients. It was very easy to lose sight of a client's personalized path. The clinical demands often created distractions from another and more important point: the client's desires. There was something in the unique and unconventional way I was called to work with Carole that gave me space to reframe and breathe freely. From this space, we were able to build a service delivery model that was client centered, with the main importance being Carole's connected communication. Our partnership allowed Carole to access her inner self and how she wanted to convey herself to the world. My experience with Carole encouraged me to rethink the term "functional communication" as embracing something larger, a client's "life goal."

Now as I see Carole emerging as a memoir and poetry writer, I reflect back on our process, asking myself how did she get here? Is there something we can take from her personal journey to improve service delivery to help others like her reach their highest personalized communication potential? I'm not sure I have all the answers, but there are some reflections that stand out along our way. As a professional I saw important changes in my service delivery occur while working with Carole, and these changes look vastly different from those required by standard clinical practice. For starters, she was my only client. This translated into fewer daily time pressures and allowed me to embrace the challenges that surfaced in my service delivery. By having the time to embrace these challenges I was able to open myself to new perspectives about what my role as speech therapist was in supporting her personal goals.

The most critical block that emerged was the prejudice that "the clinician knows best." I was faced with having to look closely at what to do if my plan as clinician, rooted in science, didn't meet the client's desires. In this case, Carole's desire was to start therapy working on her oral speech four years after her aneurysm. I realized I was competing against what scientific studies at the time were suggesting was the best course of treatment for Carole. What I found is that as much as therapists need evidence-based practice and science, we need some freedom to evoke inner creativity and communication. When we hold too tight to outcomes, getting caught in the trap of measurability, what are we ignoring and blocking from being created? My point is not to say that scientific measures are not essential in therapy. The question is, how much influence do these measures alone have on addressing the whole wellbeing of the client? Whole communication best results when we include in the spaces of science the world of desire, with all its grace and potential. I now believe that merging desire and science best supports the whole client.

From Carole I gained the ability to look at a client from her point of view and to push the limits for the sake of inspiration, because without it therapy lacks full engagement of the client and therapist. I also noticed a shift in my goal writing that occurred because I no longer wrote my goals based on the need for third party reimbursement. As I reconsidered my need to justify services to strangers, I began to hold, less rigidly, to the tally marks and percentages of her therapy goals, and was able to refocus my attention on creating connections with and for Carole.

What became highlighted were three forms of connection: Client to Clinician, Client to Others, Client to Self. How was I able to communicate better with Carole, how could others, and how could I help create a communication environment that fit how she wanted to be seen as a communicator? I came to believe it is also within the speech therapist's scope to open doors to a client's inner life. A therapist's role in this sense becomes less about teaching a particular skill, or correct sentence formation, as it is about tapping into an even larger question: What gives this client purpose and reason to communicate?

When this deep core is found within a client, inspiration leads the journey toward new ways of communicating in the world. And goal writing takes on a more organic and spontaneous flow. The client is guiding the journey and the clinician is using tools and skills to best help the client achieve goals. The map of how a therapist gets to an end unfolds as the therapist follows the passion of the client. So in Carole's example when the memoir and poetry became the target of our time together, there was a plethora of goals I could assess naturally. Each chapter she wrote of her memoir provided great writing samples of her word forms, phrases, sentences, and organization. Each preparation for the next chapter of her memoir was motivating, while providing an organic glimpse into the skills she had learned or still needed to develop. The whole goal process shifted from an external focus—proof of progression of skills in order to get insurance coverage—to an internal focus that was client centered, the achievement of Carole's life goal of writing a memoir and poetry.

This leads to the final professional observation, the need to broaden the scope of functional communication beyond necessary day-to-day needs to address deeper needs. My experience with Carole got me questioning whether the functional communication goals we create with a client are based on the narrow structures and strictures of the system in which they are living. Can we help create a broader lens that takes clients beyond daily routines to the wider world? Maybe some are able to successfully accomplish this, even given the demands within our current systems. But my experience was that it took, to some degree, freedom from such a system to liberate Carole's desire to communicate.

For Carole progress toward writing a memoir and poetry came after her everyday communication needs were met. In observing Carole's difficult journey to regain her voice through story writing and poetry, I noticed something else. For Carole to write a memoir and poetry it took patience and time. And over time her abilities grew as her confidence and skills emerged, as large or as little as these triumphs were. She had supportive family and friends to cheer on her successes and provide encouragement. As she gained power over her communication in new ways from successfully saying new words, to writing emails, to redefining her poetry writing style around her current ability, she became empowered. It was this empowerment that seemed to let her inner essence emerge, as if the time to reveal her inner world had finally arrived. Throughout the editing process I was able to witness the healing that this experience of writing a memoir held for Carole.

Each time she read the memoir she eased into a space of healing where the past and present merged and created new ground. Over time the tears that overcame her as she read her own words describing the physical insults her body endured with the shooting and aneurysm began to be replaced with a soft smile and a calm body exuding peace.

When I asked Carole if a few years ago she ever expected to write a memoir or poetry, she shook her head and said "No." Then with her deep and infectious laugh she bellowed, "I'm proud! I did it!"

Writing One of Carole's Dreams

The exchange transcribed below illustrates Carole's writing process and demonstrates the ways in which she and I collaborated through a series of questions and answers to develop clear and cohesive narratives.

Carole: My dream, many times, Shamu. There was dressage test. We knew. Orval and Hans were there. I'm forever peace and Heaven. Ending.
Anne: Do you want this to go at the end of your memoir?
Carole: Uh-huh, last chapter.
I probed for further understanding.
Anne: Was the dream recurring?
Carole: Yes.
Anne: Can you put that in a complete sentence?
Carole: I had a dream with Shamu, Orval, Hans and me.
Anne: How can we state that the dream happened many times?
Carole: Repeating.
Anne: How does this sentence sound: "I had a dream with Shamu, Orval, Hans and me, it kept repeating."
Carole: No.

Anne: How about: "I had a repetitive dream with Shamu, Orval, Hans and me."

Carole: Uh-huh.

Anne: Where were you in the dream?

Carole: Um, (unintelligible word. Carole, unprompted, grabbed pen to spell and vocalize the word for me). Fairgrounds.

Anne: Was everyone in the ring?

Carole: No, me and Shamu.

Anne: Where was everyone else?

Carole: I don't know.

Anne: So, you were unaware of them because you were riding?

Carole: Uh-huh.

Anne: What were you doing in the ring?

Carole: Trotting.

Anne: Can you give me more? Was it a competition or a show?

Carole: Show. Cantering.

Anne: Oh, you were trotting and cantering?

Carole: Uh-huh.

Anne: Let's put it into a sentence: "I and Shamu, riding dressage show, trotting and cantering." I think I have it now. But is "I and Shamu" how we should start the sentence, or should it be, "Shamu and I"?

Carole: Uh-huh, Shamu and I.

Anne: So I have: "Shamu and I were trotting and cantering in a dressage show." Should we add "where" to that sentence?

Carole: Uh-huh. Fairgrounds.

Anne: So now we have: "Shamu and I were trotting and cantering in a dressage show at the fairgrounds." Where does Hans fit in, Carole?

Carole: Because coaching me and Orval was, um, horse blanket.

Anne: What action was Orval doing? We are missing a verb. We have Hans *coaching* and Orval with a noun, *blanket*, but we don't know what he was doing with the blanket.

Carole: Holding on.

Anne: Did he put it on and off or do you just remember him holding on to the blanket?

Carole: (to the choice holding onto the blanket) Uh.
Anne: Was he watching you?
Carole: Uh, watching me.
Anne: Where?
Carole: Bleachers.
Anne: Let me read everything we have so far: "I had a repetitive dream with Shamu, Orval, Hans and me. Shamu and I were trotting and cantering in a dressage show at the fairgrounds. Hans was coaching me and Orval was sitting in the bleachers holding my horse blanket." I want to get some feeling into it. Do you remember your feelings in the ring?
Carole: I was peaceful riding.
Anne: Was it important to your peacefulness that Hans and Orval were there?
Carole: Uh-huh.
Anne: Do you want to add that? "I was peaceful riding knowing Orval and Hans were there with me."
Carole: Uh-huh. Uh-huh … and I was in heaven.
Anne: Were you physically in heaven, or the expression "I was in heaven?"
Carole: (To the choice that she was physically in heaven) Uh-huh.
Anne: So now we have: "I had a repetitive dream with Shamu, Orval, Hans and me. Shamu and I were trotting and cantering in a dressage show at the fairgrounds. Hans was coaching me and Orval was sitting in the bleachers holding my horse blanket. I was in Heaven."
Carole: Capital, capital, heaven.
Anne: Is that it?
Carole: And then, Amen.

Carole, her dream in her own words—

> I would like to write three books:
> My memoir, entitled *Shamu*,
> and two horse novels,
> *Splash* and *Solemn*.

Carole with Wade's Falcon

Love Song
by Rainer Maria Rilke

How can I keep my soul in me, so that
it doesn't touch your soul? How can I raise
it high enough, past you, to other things?
I would like to shelter it, among remote
lost objects, in some dark and silent place
that doesn't resonate when your depths resound.
Yet everything that touches us, me and you,
takes us together like a violin's bow,
which draws one voice out of two separate strings.
Upon what instrument are we two spanned?
And what musician holds us in his hand?
Oh sweetest song.

For Anne, my speech-language pathologist.
In memory of Hans, my beloved husband,
and Orval Harris Bucker.

Carole's Poems: 2013–2017

1. The Chandeliers
October 10, 2013

The Lowell's Inn has chandeliers,
Many, many chandeliers

Purple, light blue, mint green
Yellow, and orange.

Earrings, crystals, sun-catchers,
Trees,

Bouncing light
Blissful heart.

2. Knitting
October 17, 2013

Because I knit well.
I was five and I knit myself
And nobody trained me
A Breyer horse blanket with hearts
Apple green and cream
I pick up my needles and yarn and begin.

3. Horse
November 1, 2013

Galloping fast
Hooves flying
Reckless rider and horse.
Forest façade
Maybe lost, maybe found.
Galloping to heaven.

4. Balance
November 7, 2013

"Perched," too far forward,
too "laid back."
I will center myself.

5. Balance (Revised)
May 1, 2014

"Perched," too far forward,
too "laid back."
I will center myself.

Obsessive Compulsive Disorder
prisons us.

Rather, children of God,
You and me,
Freedom, united.

6. Navigate
April 3, 2014

Weather outside,
I'm tired.
Birds are eating
and they're fast
because the cold
is hungry.

7. In One's Own Time
April 10, 2014

Listening ... listening,
Quiet, air and wind.
I will ... I will pray.
I will play in silence.

8. Angels, or Evening Prayer
May 1, 2014

I love you Dad, Mom, Hans, Alma (Hans' girlfriend)
and Orval Harris.

I love you from
my heart, and my soul.

Forever and ever.

So be it!

9. Color Ferris Wheel
May 15, 2014

I dream in brown velvet
drapery.
The Ferris Wheel is barn-red
and orange-red brick
for our home.
Purple, moon blue, and olive green roses
line the driveway.
Heaven!

10. Ann
May 7, 2014

Deep purple, blue moon, lime green,
Easter eggs yellow,
and "Peace" roses peach are
keeping support.
Salute!
Express respect;
goodwill.

11. Deep Love
May 8, 2014

I see you, Angel, Orval.
I see you at midnight.
You are handsome, marvelous,
and deep.
We are strong in our love.
We are one.

12. Rainbow Angels
June 13, 2014

My bedroom is light,
and rich.

The 14 crystals, parakeets, goldfinches,
fish, butterfly, flowers,
hummingbird, and snowflakes
are glorious.

Rainbow angels are purple, light
blue, mint green, lemon yellow, and
orange.

I'm breathing;
the rainbow angels are guiding me.

The rainbow angels gala … dance!

13. My Library
July 17, 2014

Hans and I managed building
our home.

Our house was a French
Province. The bookshelves were marvelous.
Hans' were on the left side;
mine were on the right.

Hans was a disciple of horses; show jumping and
dressage; and cooking.

My passions continue to be horses, American and
English literature,
knitting, and quilting.

Our home was Hans' only.
One day I lived there!
My brain aneurysm moved me
from home; hospitals, nursing home,
Courage Center, and finally, Carol's home.

Hans died November 10, 2010.
I miss him: my husband and my coach.

Thank goodness, Nell,
Hans' student, safeguards
my books.

I'm composed; calmness.

14. The Pond
September 4, 2014

The pond reflects like a mirror.
I don't know?
Eyes frustrated?
Horse grazing?
Thunderstorm, lightning, thunder...
anxious life reflecting.

15. Happiness
October 13, 2014

With magnificence,
I touch my knitting needles. It's important I knit,

Wellbeing, I knit.
My soul is free from
work and pain.

My angels are blessing me.

My soul is brightly colored yarn.

My soul is playing in the world.

16. Hans and Football
November 20, 2014

Sunday afternoons, we watched TV.
Vikings and the opposing team.

Hans said, "The guys are glorious, and
the quarterback is graceful."

I saw myself here.
We are poised and larger in size, together.

17. For Special One
December 17, 2014

You died. Perhaps,
I was to thrust away your love: I was healing
from gun shots. My mourning cautious of
your wife and two daughters.
I love you,
You died. You were in a large
baler accident. I cried
three days. Your wife was
gracious to me at the funeral.
Large groups of people
were at the funeral.
Now, I dream of you at night.
Handsome of thought.
I love you.

18. Rejoice
January 5, 2015

In reign,
have sovereign power
Winter rules.

Like an egg having stillness and spirally;
perfection.

19. Rejoice (Revised)
January 5, 2015

Cold reigns,
sovereign power,
halting one in its tracks
Winter rules.
White covered.

Eggs fertility
having stillness,
and spirally perfection.

20. Perfect Harmony
January 8, 2015

I dream of you,
of lasting endurance.

You are my chestnut colt.
We are in the large indoor
riding arena.

Ice and snow
suddenly crash down.

The chestnut colt is rigid, and
he wildly tosses his head.

I'm nervous, but I ride deeply.

We recover and, we reclaim victory.

21. Silhouette
January 12, 2015

My teacher, Lois,
Of horses and dressage,
Died.

I saw Lois
And her Silhouette,
Black and handsome,
"Dance"
In heaven.

I dreamed it.
I was jealous!

My teacher
And her Silhouette
Are my sacred creed.

22. Dressage
January 15, 2015

Vigorously, we trot.

Lively, Shamu and I
go on; equanimity.

Shamu and I,
now, are cantering.

The "Training Level" is,
the effluent is,
the flow in the stream is
our motto.

23. Heaven
January 22, 2015

Perfect language is deeply,
deeply within,
well water.

Heaven is like a dressage level.

Dressage "levels" are training,
1,2,3,4, St. George, and Grand Prix.

As dressage, Heaven has "levels,"
deeply, deeply within,
well water.

24. Heavenly Father
February 19, 2015

I dreamt,
last night.

The worlds are the existence.
The spheres are circulatory to the sun.
The galaxies are brilliant.

I marvel at you,
Heavenly Father.

25. "Silly Putty"
June 11, 2015

Lois had an incantation,
or spell on me.

Lois and her Silhouette (horse) "Silly Putty,"
influenced me;

Silky and Shelter goes honoring them.

Silence.

26. Love Notes
July 29, 2015

I'm low,
I'm lacking of "Being"
Where my Angels,
Hans, Orval, Dad,
Mom, and Olga (Aunt Phyllis's mother) reside
and
stay with me
Your labyrinth I set my mind ....
Gloriously!

27. Dream Gaze
August 6, 2015

It's noteworthy!
Previously I only gazed at dreams
The abode of God and
the abode of angels became real.
Believe.

28. Dream Gazer
3rd Edit, August 20, 2015

It's noteworthy!
Previously, I only gazed at dreams:
Silent shots called me to
the abode of God and
the abode of angels.
I traveled within
orbits; spheres and
Heavenly bodies
becoming real
Believe!

29. The Hummingbird
September 17, 2015

With praise, I wondered
about the hummingbird.
He (she) is dancing.
His elaborate
frame bringing into being.
Delightful!
Hush! Silent.

30. Call Forth
October 1, 2015

My dreams are drifting away.
My dreams are about you.
You are my angel.
You are handsome,
with sandy brown hair, and
mustache trimmed.
Please, Heavenly Father,
amid time and distance,
let two be one.

31. Deep, Deep Love
October 29, 2015

The planets are whirling
on their axes.

The galaxies are grand…

The Creator is blessing
the world and the universe.

Deep, deep love.

32. My Church
November 5, 2015

I dream about horses.

I dream a stable is a church,
and the indoor riding ring is the nave.

The apostles are horses.

I'm listening to the horses,
thought focusing on
dressage and show jumping.

The Creator is heralding the word of the horse.

33. Dad
December 18, 2015

I'm weeping.
Dad is gone.
My dad is everything to me.

I'm mournful.

Dad is everlasting,
He is part of me.

34. My Father's Keys
February 4, 2016

With sovereign air,
Dad said, "Let's go!"

Dad's keys…

bank keys, home keys, car keys, and golf locker keys,
whirled, jiggled and jingled.

I love Dad's whistle,
in step.

I love Dad's woven bounce.

"Let's go!"

35. Lois
March 10, 2016

Lois was a champion.
Lois was a horsewoman.

She was skinny, and
Lois was "leggy."

Lois was a thoroughbred!

36. Lois (Revised)
March 24, 2016

Lois was a horsewoman.
Lois was thin and
Lois was "leggy."
Lois was a champion.

Lois was a dressage instructor and
Lois was a thoroughbred lady.
Lois was my champion.

37. Testimony
April 21, 2016

Hans was dying;
colon cancer.
How frail life is.

I witnessed Hans sail away.
Hans and I loved and were loyal.
How frail life is.

38. Valor
May 12, 2016

Deep of the night,
the crescent moon
was waxing.

The stars were thick
and bright.

I gaze dreamily.
I'm hopeful.

39. Three Belly Buttons
May 19, 2016

I'm special because of
my three belly buttons:

one natural,
two artificial.

I'm a survivor: a coma.

I'm proud of
my three belly buttons.

40. Outflow and Within
June 16, 2016

The river is flowing, and
the sandbar is reclaiming.

I'm a sexual being.
Perfect harmony.

Perfect outflow and
perfect within.

41. Outflow and Within (Revised)
July 1, 2016

The river is flowing, and
the sandbar is reclaiming itself.

I'm a sexual being; and
in the perfect harmony

I'm centering myself;
perfect outflow and
perfect within.

42. Soliloquy
July 15, 2016

I dreamed of Soliloquy.
"Solo," Soliloquy was a bay, 16.2 hands,
and slender.

He was a lady's mount,
but he was ruined.

I patted softly on his neck,
I was reaching to "Solo."
I was his voice, he was mine,
Soliloquy.

43. Shamu
August 25, 2016

Shamu was a tragedy.
Shamu was an abused thoroughbred,
17.0 hands, and beautiful.

Hans' stable was ideal.
Hans, Wayne, who was the stable man,
and me controlled everything.

But, I was sick: a brain aneurysm,
that took me away.
Hans was worried about me.
Shamu was sold ….
Shamu was abused again, and "put down".

Years pass … Hans and Wayne pass.

I'm dreaming that they are all together in Heaven,
ideally.

Thinking in Poems

Sent from Carole's iPad

I am writing poems two days a week, now. My mind thinks in poems, which is different; before it was just survival.

My poems come to me in pictures. Not like a movie. More like one big scene and I search for the words to describe it.

Nature is my inspiration. I deeply see nature. When I look at a bird it is more than just a bird. It awakens me. I see symbols, I feel emotions, I hear the bird. It gets my natural flow going.

I'm learning how to use new software on my iPad that helps me type a bit faster and reads my poems back to me.

I have future pieces I want to write. They are about dressage, show jumping and more poems. I used to show-jump and ride dressage. Those times were thrilling. There is salvation from suffering when I write about that time.

I think about Hans, Orval, Mom, Dad, and horses, always!

Carole Jayne Stoa Senn
January 2017

Special Acknowledgment from Carole

I want to thank those who directly helped to make this book happen, and my family, care team and friends for their continued encouragement, support and love.

To my memoir team editor Emilio DeGrazia, Tom Driscoll, managing editor of Shipwreckt Books Publishing Company, book design advisor Jill Krase, Monica DeGrazia, for her careful editorial advice, and my writing companion, Anne Gerber: thank you for your belief in me and for giving of your time. I couldn't have done it without you.

Thank you to my wonderful family, especially my late husband Hans Senn, my mother Merle Stoa, my father Arnold Erick Stoa, my brother Tom Stoa and his wife Christine Stoa, my brother Jim Stoa and Gail Christiannsen, and my sister Helen DelVecchio, and to Aunt Phyllis Thysell, Brian Thysell, Nancy Thysell and countless cousins, nieces and nephews who share their family stories and connect me to their lives. Thank you for your support, visits, gifts, and letters over the years.

A special thank you is due to each of my care team members and friends: Carol Warren, Jody Hop, Ann Bleeker, Emily Bleeker, Orval Harris Bucker, Wayne Wood, Nell Kromhout Alt, Dillion McGrath, Sabon Crook, Lynn and Royce Curtis, Sandra Knaeble, Alice Knaeble, Jan Fisk, Nan Cowin, Cindy Hansen, MerryLea Slowkowski, Linda Schmitt, Julia Engelman, Karen Olszewskie, Madeline Brugler. Thank you for your care and companionship and for teaching me to trust. You each have a place in the different stories of the many chapters of my life.

—Carole Jayne Stoa Senn

Lost Lake **Folk Art**

SHIPWRECKT BOOKS PUBLISHING COMPANY
Minnesota

www.ingramcontent.com/pod-product-compliance
Lightning Source LLC
Chambersburg PA
CBHW022111090426
42743CB00008B/802